"Last Days" Timeline

Volume #2: The Prophecy of The Tame and Wild Olive Trees

- For Latter-day Saints -

By James T. Prout

© 2019 James T. Prout
All rights reserved.

No part of this book may be reproduced in any form whatsoever without prior written permission from the author.

The Church of Jesus Christ of Latter-day Saints does not endorse this work. The opinions and views expressed herein belong solely to the author. Permission for the use of images, photos, and sources is also solely the responsibility of the author.

ISBN-13: 978-0-9985443-2-8

Version 1.8

The Primary Purpose of This Work

The primary purpose of this work is to demonstrate with precision, what the future holds using the scriptures themselves. Not dreams, not visions, and not extra-curricular prophecies. Ranging from next week - to the Second Coming of the Lord Jesus Christ.

So, you may know how to prepare your family physically and spiritually for the exact events directly ahead.

This specific work deals with Jacob Chapter 5: The Allegory of The Tame and Wild Olive Trees by Zenos

This timeline of the *last-day* events in prophecy will focus on the: Who, What, Where, When, Why, and sometimes How. For a Timeline to be CONCISE, we must focus most on What, Where, and When or … **What happens, When does it happen, and Where does it happen.** The Who, Why, and How, will be addressed in the Appendices. This will include much of the identification of the symbolism. Remember, we are focused on a timeline in this work.

This is a "living work". This is a book to keep on your shelf for the rest of your life. Refer to it often as a reference. Share it with your friends. Stay connected with me through the website www.LastDaysTimeline.com.

As new material becomes available, I will update you and continue the struggle for **truth**.

I want the truth of a good timeline. That is all.

Nothing more than the truth, and nothing less than the truth.

Discover
The "Last Days" Timeline Series

Go to www.LastDaysTimeline.com

…and more to come.

Table of Contents

ACKNOWLEDGEMENTS 7

How to Read this Book 7

SECTION 1: The Fall of Ancient Israel and The "Times of The Gentiles" Begins 17

    1: The True Prophet That Nobody Knows? 18

    2. Israel Is Growing Old in The Land and Adopting The Religion of Baal 22

    3. What Did Jesus Say to The Children of Lehi? 40

    4. Jesus Continues the Sermon to The Children of Lehi As a Commandment Of The Father About The Gentiles 43

SECTION 2: The NEW Gentile Converts Come Into The Church of Jesus Christ And Scattered Israel Is Flourishing At The Same Time 46

    5. Gentiles Begin to Produce Good Fruit 47

    6. Paul – The Apostle of The Gentiles 51

    7. What Happens to The NEW Gentile Christians After Paul is Martyred? 65

    8. What Do The Lost 10 Tribes Look Like At 33-200 A.D.? 69

    9. The 33 A.D. Visit of Jesus To Work With The Lost 10 Tribes And Have Them Record His Words as Scripture To Deepen Their Root Systems 79

SECTION 3: The Gentile's Great Apostasy Along With Israel's Great Apostasy At The Same Time – No Good Fruit 86

    10. What Happens After The Gentile's Great Apostasy? How Does The Master/Lord Want to Deal With This Problem? 87

    11. What Is The Future Gentile's Stumbling Block That Nephi Saw in 600 B.C.? 94

    12. Was The Gentile Great Apostasy Prophesied? 108

    13. What is Happening to The Lost 10 Tribes of Israel in 1820 AD? 115

    14. An Enemy Hath Done This 121

SECTION 4: The Plan For Restoration Is Presented 132

15. The High Branches Have Overcome The Roots. How Does That Happen? ... 133

16. The Idea is Set. Let's Discover What The Plan is For Our Future Beyond 2019 ... 136

SECTION 5: The Plan For Restoration Is Begun ... *140*

17. The Last Days Restoration of Jesus Christ's True Church in The Vineyard Has Begun ... 141

18. This Last Work in The Vineyard Is a Big Job – Call For Some Help ... 150

19. How Will The Father Eliminate The Wicked People in The Gentile Nations That Currently Cumber The Ground of His Earth? ... 153

20. How Shall They Be "One"? ... 159

21. It Works! The Nation of Zion Succeeds in Producing Natural Fruit From All 12 of Israel's Branches. The Unbelieving Gentile Branches Are Removed and Burned. ... 164

22. The Natural Fruit Has Been Restored – The 144,000 Have Been Successful ... 167

23. The Great 1000 Year Millennium Appears Before Us ... 169

24. The End of The Millennium – More Bad Fruit ... 171

25. How Can I Use This Information To Prepare My Family? ... 176

Appendix 1: The Teachings of Zenos ... *179*

Appendix 2: Recognizing The Great Apostasy ... *182*

Appendix 3: Other Vineyards and Tree Principles in the Scriptures ... *227*

Appendix 4: Times of the Gentiles ... *234*

ACKNOWLEDGEMENTS

No work of substantial importance is accomplished by one person. It is always a team effort. This is a big THANK YOU to those that helped with image artwork creation, editing, and doctrine correctness.

I express deep gratitude toward my wife and my Heavenly Father. Without the support of both, this work would not have taken place.

How to Read this Book

This book is written in several segments. It was not written to be a novel to be read from front to back. This book was written to be more of a resource of all available material and prophecy on the subject of *Zenos' Prophecy of The Tame and Wild Olive Trees*.

This book was also written to be very precise, without a lot of fluff. Your author has tried to keep the words to a minimum. That is very strange in the world of book writing. But, in the world of understanding and knowledge, if an idea can be stated simply, then that is usually best.

Prophecy is defined as information from God about the future, given to mankind.

No one man that has a corner on the market of prophecy, except our Father in Heaven. The living prophet of God has the right to prophesy officially for the whole church. This book is the assembly of all things and topics surrounding the future as stated by the prophets and Apostles concerning the *Prophecy of The Tame and Wild Olive Trees*.

This work of The "Last Days" Timeline Series is unique in that it is a lifelong work. Once deciding to write a book on revelation and prophecy of the future, I came to the sudden knowledge that it is a never-ending work. The topic keeps expanding as new insights into old scriptures come into view; also the events of the last days keep getting fulfilled. So, I have dedicated the remainder of my life to updating this book series and this project with the most up-to-date information for the reader.

As a lifelong research project directed by the Spirit of the Almighty, I request your prayers to gain power over Satan and the darkness of mind that fills the natural man. For when this work is underway, I desire that the light of truth will wash over your mind that you may prepare physically and spiritually for the trials of fire for the Saints ahead.

This book is written to be read like an internet blog post. The main books of **The Last Days Timeline Series** will have several appendices in the back of the books and the website www.LastDaysTimeline.com. Use these notes and links to discover more on the topics mentioned in the Timeline. The Timeline will not discuss subtopics in-depth. A precise timeline is what we want. The rest will be in the Appendixes.

Format and Printing

This book is written in web format style, to be easy to read in chunks, and easy to scan.

The book is meant to be printed inexpensively, to get the information out to the most people possible. It is not in color. The website reference link www.LastDaysTimeline.com will be placed on important images, so that you can see the **full-size** versions in color for your study. This book series resource is to be used with the website www.LastDaysTimeline.com together.

About Your Author and The Dilemma

Your author for this work is James T Prout.

I am a veteran of marketing and business leadership and the use of the written word has been with me during my whole career. I have built and sold several businesses and love doing that. My mind works well in that field.

The #1 skill I have developed that has influenced me the most in writing this book has been the reading of 10-15 pages of a good book every day. I have been reading like that since 1997. When the total number of good books, good documentaries and audiobooks are added to the mix, I regularly cover 120-160 books, documentaries, and audiobooks each year. That is a lot of digested materials on a lot of different subjects. I am a good student and I take notes on what I study under the direction of the Spirit.

There was no plan to write a book series at all. I like reading them, not writing them.

Recently, there was a prophecy-last-days book written that I gleaned much good information and I felt edified. The next book I read was a "dreams and visions" book. It claimed many things that were against the scriptures. Yet, the author claimed their vision was "the truth" and that the scriptures were "misunderstood". I was shocked at how far off the vision's timeline was from the scriptures. This should not be.

I wanted a timeline that was straight-forward and answered the question of "What is the reliable last-days timeline from scripture?" A timeline that is good enough for my own family and friends to know what to prepare for *next*.

This work surely has my opinion woven into the fabric of the pages. However, I will do my best to state what is my opinion and theory and to keep the reader on solid footing with the research, rather than project the research to fit my own theories.

Elder Boyd K. Packer of the Quorum of the 12 Apostles said this about the hidden treasures of the scriptures:

> (The Mystery of Life Nov 1983)
> "For His own reasons, the Lord provides answers to some questions, with pieces placed here and there throughout the

scriptures. We are to find them; we are to **earn** them. In that way sacred things are hidden from the insincere."

I want truth and **only truth** will do for me…and I feel that many Latter-day Saints want truth as well.

(D&C 93:24)
"24 And truth is knowledge of things **as they are**, and **as they were**, and **as they are to come**;"

Truth of the present, the past, and the future.

Sources and Emphasis Fonts

I will use *all* the sources that are known to me at this time. They are rated from very authentic down to less believable. However, we will include them *all* and then research under the direction of the Spirit to find the answers…..as to what sources should be added to the Timeline of Future Last Days Events.

This is an ongoing work and will be updated regularly. When new sources or materials become available to me, this work will be expanded.

In the scriptural quotes and other quotes, I have added emphasis in **bold** and with **bold underline** for extra important emphasis. And any author explanatory additions to the scriptures are put in [brackets].

Authority for Conclusions

I have authority only for my own words and family. I have no authority for The Church of Jesus Christ of Latter-day Saints in general. If there is a statement by one who has authority from The Church that is opposite or contrary to what I have stated, their statement should supersede.

What is the Purpose of Good Research?

Good research should get to the nitty-gritty of the topic and to paint the topic in a simplistic light, so that all readers can understand the topic.

If one reads the books written by Albert Einstein, his expansive ideas and concepts of atomic energy and waves are distilled into simple concepts that are easily understood by the common man. Simplicity was one of his greatest gifts.

The sequence of last-days events will get better as time passes. There will be frequent updates to this book and the website www.LastDaysTimeline.com will hold much of the new information before it goes into the next edition of this work.

Identifying Prophecy is Like "Hitting an Archery Target"

Much of what is written in the scriptures and recorded in the written Word of God is interpreted through our own frame of reference. We all have a frame of reference. Our minds insert it **before** we draw conclusions on the information we have collected with our 5 senses.

This means that our Frame of Reference prevents us from interpreting ideas and concepts the way that our perfected God interprets the same ideas and concepts.

(Isaiah 55:9) "For as the heavens are higher than the earth, **so are my ways higher than your ways, and my thoughts than your thoughts.**"

(creative commons)

Reading prophecy of the future is always subjective. It can be no other way. It's like hitting around the center on this archery target. However, real history is like hitting the bulls-eye. When the events of the last days come to pass, it becomes history, not prophecy any longer. We will all have the opportunity of seeing how history is played out.

I Do Not Believe in a Truncated Short Timeline – This Stuff Takes Years

After looking at the compilation of knowledge on the subject of future prophecy and the events on the Timeline, it is quite clear that many of these things take years and decades to happen. Rome wasn't built in a day.

I do not believe in a truncated short timeline. As you will discover from the research, many of these things take years to come to pass. Christ's second coming is not going to happen tomorrow. But it will happen…as the events on the Timeline come to pass one-by-one.

Always Include the Spirit

Every church book and author I have ever read has always said to "pray for the inspiration of the Spirit as you read my book."

Yet, all of these books on last-days events have conflicting material and author interpretations that are going to be wrong.

THE PROBLEM: Literally, they all say their conclusions have been sought by the Spirit and are correct. However, the authors of "prophecy last-days books" are coming to different conclusions as to what the symbol images mean and the timeline of how they fit together.

I do not believe that God the Father is the author of confusion. I do not believe that all the Christian churches in the world, with all their varying understandings of doctrine, to **all** be correct. The problem is the same with prophecy-last-days book writers.

I do not claim any special "hidden knowledge" or dream nor vision. I simply have all the same material available to me that you the reader have.

Please pray for the Holy Spirit as you read this book, *and* also pray for me that the work of recording prophecy of last-day events may be correct and <u>*tightly aligned with the real history of the future events*</u> as they unfold as have been revealed.

I do *not* claim to have it right the first time. This is an ongoing work and will be added upon as new information comes into view. New information *will* change my opinions over time. However, I am committed to this work of recording the prophecies of the last-days from all authoritative and semi-authoritative sources and presenting them to you, the reader, for a lifetime.

This is a collaborative work. I am asking **directly** for you, the reader, to participate in the ideas surrounding The Last Days Timeline Series. After you read this work and read additional work that is on this book's website www.LastDaysTimeline.com, please contact me and share your ideas... thus expanding this work. Thank you.

Why The Prophecy of The Tame and Wild Olive Trees as The 2nd Book in The "Last Days" Timeline Series?

During the heated political time of early 2017, I was reading The Book of Mormon with my family and reached Jacob Chapter 5.

The Last Days Timeline – Volume 1 had already been printed by about 2 months. Yet, I kept seeing more prophecy and more information about the future; things that I had not deeply touched-on before. In fact, the prophecies are everywhere.

Jacob chapter 5 is a very under-rated source of prophecy.

This is the longest chapter in the Book of Mormon and the longest set of fictional imagery in all the scriptures. It deserves our full attention.

Therefore, if you will stay with me, we will explore the whole **prophecy** that Zenos gave titled: The Allegory of The Tame and Wild Olive Trees.

You will get an advanced sneak peek at the depths of this mysterious prophecy of the future. Let's solve the riddles together.

SECTION 1: The Fall of Ancient Israel and The "Times of The Gentiles" Begins

Original Artwork

1: The True Prophet That Nobody Knows?

Who was Zenos, really?

Was he a prophet of God? Why don't we have his work in the Old Testament?

If Zenos' work was scuttled, why did they do it?

To understand the answers to these questions, we must learn about Zenos and what he wrote.

Only then, can we understand the situation surrounding Zenos and the specific elements of the prophecy itself.

The Background: Who, What, Where, When, Why

Who recorded the prophecy? Zenos wrote the Allegory of The Tame and Wild Olive Trees. Zenos is a lost prophet in the Old Testament. We know this because in Nephi and Jacob's day (600-550BC) Zenos was included on the Brass Plates. (See Appendix 1: Teachings of Zenos)

What is the prophecy about? This passage of Jacob chapter 5 is an allegory. An allegory is a fictional story that relates important hidden truths. This allegory in Jacob 5 relates a prophetic timeline of the future that is **way ahead** of Nephi and Jacob's time of 600-550 B.C.

Where was it given: The prophet Zenos was an Old Testament prophet pre-600 B.C. There are no other details about **where** Zenos lived or when he received the revelation. Jacob recited this parable out loud and then explained it to his people while in The Land of Nephi; North of the Land of First Inheritance.

When was it given: Zenos lived pre-600 B.C. Jacob read the writings of Zenos from the Plates of Brass which contained our Old Testament plus more books. These writings of Zenos pre-date the Nephites. Thus, the prophecies were very far forward from Zenos' day. And only after Nephi's written revelation did Zenos' writings make sense as applied to the Gentiles' interactions with the Tribes of Israel of the future. (See Appendix 1: Teachings of Zenos)

Why was it given: Mormon included most of the writings of the founders of the Nephite society. The big 3 were Lehi, Nephi, and Jacob. These first 3 leaders successfully taught doctrine centered in Christ in an Old Testament era. Mormon appreciated that. This small Book of Jacob was included because of the church sermons that Jacob gave to his people. Including Jacob's telling of The Allegory of The Tame and Wild Olive Trees to his people, and his explanation of it. It's all about the Gentiles, which Mormon was well aware would inhabit the Promised Land of the Americas.

Let Us See How Jacob Introduces Zenos' Prophecy
Jacob is providing scriptural evidence of the future advent of the Messiah that will come and atone for the sins of His faithful followers. Yet, Jacob knows the prophecies that the Jews, from which the

Nephites came, will reject the Messiah and crucify him. Nephi saw it. Jacob believed it. (See: Jacob 4:12-14)

So, how is it possible that the Jews will reject their Messiah; the very person they are waiting for? And yet still be given a chance to accept him later?

> (Jacob 4:15-18 accents added)
> "**15** And now I, Jacob, am **led on by the Spirit unto prophesying**; for I perceive by the workings of the Spirit which is in me, that **by the stumbling** of the Jews they will reject the stone upon which they might build and have safe foundation.
> **16** But behold, according to the scriptures, this stone shall become the great, and the last, and the only sure foundation, upon which the Jews can build.
> **17** And now, my beloved, **how is it possible** that these, **after** having rejected the sure foundation, **can ever** build upon it, **that it may become** the head of their corner?
> **18** Behold, my beloved brethren, **I will unfold this mystery unto you**; if I do not, by any means, get shaken from my firmness in the Spirit, and stumble because of my over anxiety for you."

Learning Points:
  A. Jacob has the Spirit of Prophecy as he teaches this congregation of Nephites.
  B. The Jews will reject their Messiah.
  C. Yet, **after** the rejection of Jesus of Nazareth in 33 A.D., the Jews will **once again** build upon Jesus as the long-awaited

Messiah. Jacob is looking far into the future with this prophecy; as this has not been fulfilled as of 2019.

D. The Prophecy of The Tame and Wild Olive Trees **is the evidence** that Jacob is offering to answer the question, "**How can the Jews build their religious foundations upon Jesus.**" Inadvertently, Jacob also demonstrates **when** this prophecy is fulfilled in the history of the world.

2. Israel Is Growing Old in The Land and Adopting The Religion of Baal

All timelines have a beginning and an ending. The characters may live before or after those points, but the story itself has a beginning and an ending.

What Time Period Does The Prophecy Show First?

When is the opening scene of Zenos' allegorical prophecy? This will also give the reader a timeframe as to when this amazing prophet Zenos lived. (See Appendix: Teachings of Zenos)

> (Jacob 5:1-4 accents added)
> "**1** Behold, my brethren, do ye not remember to have read the words of the prophet **Zenos**, which he spake unto the house of Israel, saying:
> **2** Hearken, O ye house of Israel, and hear the words of me, **a prophet** of the Lord.
> **3** For behold, thus saith the Lord, I will liken thee, **O house of Israel, like unto a tame olive tree**, which a man took and nourished in his **vineyard**; and it **grew**, and **waxed old**, and **began to decay**.

4 And it came to pass that **the master** of the vineyard went forth, and he saw that his olive tree **began** to decay; and he said: I will prune it, and dig about it, and nourish it, that perhaps it may shoot forth **young and tender branches**, and it perish not."

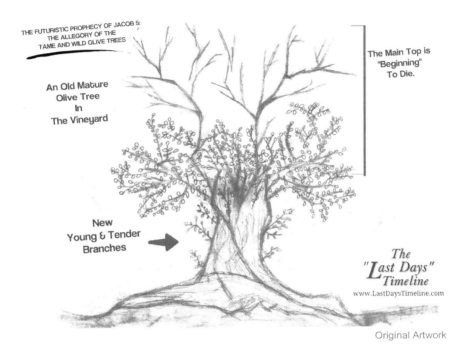

Learning Points:
  A. Zenos is the prophet that originally wrote this allegory.
  B. **The House of Israel** = the Tame Olive Tree.
  C. In this opening period of the prophecy, Israel is decaying. The tree is **beginning** to die. The time period we are looking at is when Israel as a nation has been in the holy land for many

centuries. **Before** the Northern Kingdom of Israel (10 tribes) was carried away into Assyria in 721 BC. **Before** the Jews were carried away into Babylon in 597 BC. Note: This timeline identification is used in the next few verses.

   a. **Author's Analysis**: This prophecy suggests that the "tree **beginning to perish**" timeframe began at least as far back as the division of the Northern Kingdom of Israel and the Southern Kingdom of Judah. Additionally, many of the Old Testament prophets spoke of the evils that went on in Israel during this few hundred year period. Most of the problems for the Northern Kingdom of Israel and the Southern Kingdom of Judah related to taking up the **idol religion of Baal** from their neighbors **the Canaanites**. God foresaw through the ages and predicted this would happen if Joshua didn't clear out the land of the current residents. Israel would take up the idol worship of their neighbors. Baal was the **god of war** and the **god of prosperity**. Eventually, the worship of Baal became authorized and promoted by **the Government** of the land. Then **sexual practices** were put on display in the temples of Baal. Then **homosexuality** followed next. Finally the ritual **sacrifice of children** in the fires in front of the statues of Baal. All for the sake of "prosperity."

D. The Master of the Vineyard is not yet identified. That will come later.

E. The Master **plans a strategy** to enliven Israel including:

a. **pruning** - (snipping undesired branches to stimulate growth). This is akin to helping **grow the size and population** of the desired branches.
   b. **digging about it** - (softening the soil so the root system can get wider and collect moisture). This is akin to growing or enlarging **what the roots represent**.
   c. **nourishing** - (with fertilizer). This is akin to **giving power and nutrition** to all parts of the tree to gain strength.
F. The plan is to do the work necessary to (maybe) have Israel shoot forth **young and tender branches**. These new branches will ultimately preserve the tree of Israel itself.
G. **The Vineyard = the landmasses of earth**. This becomes apparent in a few more verses when the branches are grafted in far-flung places of ground all over the vineyard.

Author's Analysis:

Some prophecy writers may suppose that this Allegory of The Tame and Wild Olive Trees is 100% spiritual. In other words…the identification of the elements in the story are all spiritual. This is not so.

Jacob was using this future prophetic allegory to explain a real point to the people…that one day the Jews will come to know their Messiah.

Some elements are spiritual and some are physical. This means we are dealing with real people in real history.

> Others have asked an important question, "What did this Olive Tree look like when it was in its prime? Or when was Israel in its prime?"
>
> That portion of the Earth's Timeline is not represented in this prophecy. However, since the prophecy opens in a time when Israel is in decay, but the dead top branches have not yet been burned; then the answer as to when Israel was in its prime was when there was **just 1 kingdom**, it hadn't split yet. And also when the **Reign of the Judges** were taking place, plus the first few generally righteous kings. That would be the prime of the olive tree and the prime of Israel's existence.

What Is The Vineyard?

The Vineyard of the Lord is all the landmasses of the Earth. I've heard it said that the Vineyard is the universe or the galaxy. I don't believe that to be the case.

However, there is nothing wrong with multiple vineyards of work. As there are multiple earths like our own populated with God's spirit children, then there would be multiple vineyards.

I performed a search in the Doctrine and Covenants, and it appears that there are over 29 references to "working in the vineyard."

What Did The Master Do For His Olive Tree Before The Top Died?

These precious moments in the prophecy show that The Master has always taken good care of his people. Even when the people thought He neglected them.

> (Jacob 5:5-7 accents added)
> " **5** And it came to pass that he **pruned it**, and **digged about it**, and **nourished it** according to **his word**.
> **6** And it came to pass that <u>after many days</u> it began to put forth somewhat a little, **young and tender branches**; but behold, <u>the main top</u> thereof began to **perish**.
> **7** And it came to pass that **the master of the vineyard saw it**, and he said unto **his servant**: It **grieveth me** that I should lose this tree; wherefore, go and pluck the branches **from a wild olive tree**, and bring them hither unto me; and we will **pluck off those main branches** which are beginning to wither away, and we will **cast them into the fire** that they may be burned."

Learning Points:

A. The Master himself personally did the work on the olive tree of Israel. All according to his plan, that was stated earlier. The Servant is not working on the scene yet, until Verse 7.

B. Much time went by. The plan worked. The olive tree of Israel did indeed put forth young and tender branches.

C. The main established top of Israel, including the other branches began to die. This implies the leadership of both the Northern Kingdom of Israel and eventually the Southern Kingdom of

Judah were corrupted during this time period of a few hundred years.

D. (v7) The **Servant** of The Master of the vineyard is introduced here. The Servant works with the Master, **under his direction** (clue #1). The identification of both characters of the story will be identified shortly...when more evidence has presented itself.

E. The **Master is grieving** for Israel; so, he creates a new plan. To graft wild olive tree branches where the old branches currently are. Then at the same time, to take the new young and tender branches to split them up all over the Vineyard.

F. The old branches are burned. **Only the young tender branches survive the day.** This implies that the old leadership who were corrupted were mostly killed off through the assault of Assyria and the assault of Babylon. And that some keepers of the tribal Israelite family-lines were carried away and transplanted. (More on this to come.)

G. The wild olive branches to be grafted into Israel is in the planning stages, at this time. It happens **after** the burning of the old branches, and **after** the disbursing of the young and tender branches. **The wild olive branches = the Gentiles**. (Gentiles being consistently defined as Caucasian Europeans. See Appendix in *The "Last Days" Timeline* – Volume 1 – Gentiles, Heathen and Israel)

Author's Analysis:

This is where our initial 721 B.C. time-frame setting of this first scene appears to be a little "off" with real history. Because the major Gentile transplants into the tree happened much later than 721 B.C.

There are 4 possibilities:
- A. The time period we are discussing is not 721 B.C. – 597 B.C. But is more like 721 B.C. to 45 A.D.
   Peter and Paul were the first to be commanded to bring Gentiles into the Church of Jesus Christ. To my knowledge, Gentiles were not allowed into the Jewish religion. (See Appendix: Times of the Gentiles)
- B. (possibility) Ephraim seems to have rebelled during the long trip North and left many Ephraimites in Europe, as the rest of the body kept going North. (as shown in quote below)
- C. (speculation only) When the Lost 10 Tribes were making their way North after escaping and being led out of Assyria, they could have picked up some European Gentiles as converts along the way. This idea seems far fetched to me, given their constant movement North.
- D. The expanded meaning of the word "Gentiles" may include other peoples surrounding Israel, other than Caucasian Europeans. However, I do not know of any other large non-Jewish groups that were adopted into Christ's Church, or the Jewish religion except during the Roman Empire period following Christ's earthly ministry.
   (See Appendix Item in *The Last Days Timeline – Volume 1*: Gentiles, Heathen, and Israelites)

The Long Trip North

The very long **1.5 year trip north** for the Lost 10 Tribes of Israel was recorded in *The "Last Days" Timeline – Volume 1 appendix*. This quote comes from the Old King James Version of The Apocrypha. It is located in the very next chapter **after** the Ezra's Eagle Prophecy.

> (2nd Esdras 13:40-46 accents added)
>
> "**40** Those are the <u>ten tribes</u>, which were carried away prisoners out of their own land in the time of Osea the king, whom Salmanasar the **king of Assyria** led away captive, and he carried them over the waters, and so came they into another land.
>
> **41** But they took this counsel among themselves, that they would leave the multitude of the heathen, and go forth **into a further country, where never mankind dwelt,**
>
> **42** That they might there **keep their statutes**, which they never kept in their own land.
>
> **43** And they entered into Euphrates by the narrow places of the river.
>
> **44** For <u>**the most High then shewed signs for them**</u>, and **held still the flood, till they were passed over.**
>
> **45** For through that country there was <u>**a great way to go**</u>, namely, of <u>**a year and a half**</u>: and the same **region is called <u>Arsareth</u>.**

> **46** Then dwelt they there **until the latter time**; and now when they shall begin to come,"

Learning Points:
A. The Lost 10 Tribes escaped Assyrian captivity and traveled 1.5 years north. In **1.5 years**, a large group traveling an average of just 7 miles per day for 6 days per week could go around 3,276 miles. (if averaging 10 miles/day then 4,680 miles).
  1. **NOTE:** The distance from Eastern Turkey (Northern area of the Assyrian Empire) to the northern tip of Norway is only 2,786 miles.
B. The group was led by The Most High on purpose. With signs ahead of them to lead them on their path north.
C. The area where they live today, until the "latter time" is called **Arsareth**.

The Lost 10 Tribes, on their way to becoming lost to the rest of the world, traveled north 1.5 years and most likely had interactions with other peoples. What those interactions were, we won't know.

Who is The Lord of The Vineyard and Who is The Servant?

This is one of the identification sections where we can see the true nature of the identities of The Master/Lord and The Servant.

> (Jacob 5:8-14 accents added)
> "**8** And behold, saith the Lord of the vineyard, **I (The**

Master/Lord) take away many of these **young and tender branches**, and I will **graft them whithersoever I will**; and it mattereth not that if it so be that **the root** of this tree will perish, I may preserve **the fruit** thereof unto myself; wherefore, I will take these young and tender branches, and I will graft them whithersoever I will.

9 Take thou the **branches** of the **wild olive tree**, and **graft them in**, in the stead thereof; and **these which I have plucked off I will cast into the fire and burn them**, that they may not cumber the ground of my vineyard.

10 And it came to pass that **the servant** of the Lord of the vineyard did according to the word of the Lord of the vineyard, and **grafted in the branches of the wild olive tree**.

11 And the Lord of the vineyard caused that it should be digged about, and pruned, and nourished, saying unto his servant: It grieveth me that I should lose this tree; wherefore, that perhaps **I might preserve the roots** thereof that they perish not, that I might **preserve them unto myself**, I have done this thing.

12 Wherefore, go thy way; **watch the tree**, and nourish it, according to my words.

13 And **these will I place in the nethermost part of my vineyard**, whithersoever **I will, it mattereth not unto thee**; and I do it that I may preserve unto myself **the natural branches of the tree**; and also, that I may lay up **fruit** thereof against the season, unto myself; for it grieveth me that I should lose this tree and the fruit thereof.

14 And it came to pass that **the Lord** of the vineyard went his way, and **hid the natural branches of the tame olive tree in**

the nethermost parts of the vineyard, some in one and some in another, according to **his** will and pleasure."

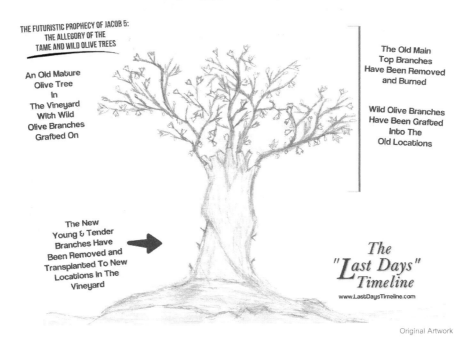

Learning Points:

A. **The Master/Lord of the Vineyard = Heavenly Father Himself**. We learn this from the next set of verses in 3rd Nephi, which demonstrates this exact scenario. The scenario is The Master/Lord hid the young and tender branches of Israel away from the knowledge of the world **and** The Servant.

B. **The Servant = Jesus Christ.** We learn this from the same scripture in 3rd Nephi. The Servant doesn't know where The Master/Lord hid Israel. Thus, The Lost 10 Tribes were hidden by The Father directly without information given to The Son, yet.

- a. **Author's Analysis**: There has been prophecy writers who claimed that The Lord of the Vineyard is Jesus Christ and that the Servant is a prophet, or prophets in general, or even a special last days servant; like The Rod, The Root, The Stem, or The Branch of Jessie. However, as we dive into the allegory further, these possible identifications melt away. (See Appendix Item in *The "Last Days" Timeline – Volume 1: The Rod, The Root, The Stem, The Branch; all of Jessie*)
- C. The Master/Lord has been working with these young and tender branches of Israel. The Servant has not been working with them **yet**. He doesn't even know where they were for a good long time. As shown in the next few verses.
- D. **The nethermost parts of the Vineyard = Very far away...to the extreme and far-flung landmasses on planet earth.**
    - a. **Author's Analysis**: The exact location will surprise billions of people upon the Earth in the last days when those Lost 10 Tribes return from their hidden location where the Father hath led them. However, if you research, then pray for confirmation; you can know.
- E. **The Roots = The scriptures and teachings from God to man**. This is demonstrated in the next few verses. (Note: if one says "The Root = The Gospel", it would be partially correct. But, the word "gospel" means different things to different people. I prefer to be precise.)
- F. **Author's Analysis: The Tree Trunk = The Church of Jesus Christ.** Because the Roots under the church are the Word of God given to man and the teachings from God to man. Also, the 12 Tribes of Israel are the branches connecting to the tree

trunk, then the trunk itself is the authorized Church of Christ. This is an author's analysis section because the tree trunk is nowhere mentioned in the allegory, other than "the tree".

G. **The Good Fruit** = (Shall be clearly defined directly below). Note that **the branches** produce the fruit.

H. The old decayed natural branches of the tame olive tree were plucked off and burned by The Master/Lord.

I. The wild olive tree branches were grafted onto the tame olive tree's structure by The Servant.

J. The Servant was also commanded to "watch the tree" for a time and dig around it, prune it and fertilize it. Remember at this point, the Roots of the scriptures and teachings are what The Master/Lord wants The Servant to protect and to nourish. **The roots** are the most important **resource** to keep alive from the original tree.

K. The Master/Lord himself, at the same time, **hid** the natural tame olive branches of Israel in the nethermost parts of the earth's landmasses and grafted those branches into other tree locations during this period of time.

L. **The Wild Olive Branches = The Gentiles.** This is the big Gentile movement into Israel by adoption, if not by direct trace family-lines. To my knowledge, this took place just after the meridian of time through the initial preaching of Paul and Peter. Approximately 40AD through 250AD-ish. Give or take. (Note: it depends upon what year the scholars peg The Great Apostasy to begin. By 380AD The Great Apostasy was well underway with *Roman Constantine The Great* declaring…the belief system of the day…as the **state religion**. See more below.)

God the Father owns this Earth. In the sacred temple ceremonies, we learn that God the Father has the plan and Jesus Christ helps in the execution of that plan as the primary collaborator.

In August 1988 in the Ensign Magazine, there was an article by Ralph E. Swiss about Zenos' allegory.

> (The Tame and Wild Olive Trees –Ensign Magazine, Aug 1988)
> "As Zenos begins the story, he defines the primary figure: the tame olive tree, which he said represents the house of Israel. He then speaks of the tree growing old and beginning to decay. From the opening verses, the love and concern of the master of the garden are evident as he seeks ways to help the tree survive and bear good fruit. (Jacob 5:4.) The lord of the vineyard and his servants may refer to the Lord Jesus Christ and his disciples, the prophets; at least Jacob seems to refer to them as such when he explains the implications of the allegory. (See Jacob 6:2–4, 8.) **Others, noting that the lord of the vineyard has a chief servant working in the vineyard, assign the role of <u>lord of the vineyard to God the Father</u>**."
> (See the whole Ensign article here: https://www.churchofjesuschrist.org/study/ensign/1988/08/the-tame-and-wild-olive-trees-an-allegory-of-our-saviors-love?lang=eng)

The Good Fruit is Glory

I assume that the fruit is the righteousness worked by the people to change their hearts toward Christ…of all 12 Tribes of Israel and later Gentiles. There could be other definitions. However, knowing what we do about the Gospel of Jesus Christ, and that the Master/Lord = God The Father, then righteous repentant people that follow The Christ is what is needed.

What is the desired result as to what God wants from his creations? Why does he labor on this Earth?

> (Moses 1:39)
> "**39** For behold, this is **my work and my glory**—to bring to pass the **immortality and eternal life of man**."

This is why the worth of souls is great in the sight of God. **Your** immortality and eternal life is **adding glory** to our Father in Heaven.

Glory is **the end result** of the creation of this earth via the Plan of Salvation.

> (Abraham 3:25-27 accents added)
> "**25** And we will prove them herewith, to see if they will **do all things whatsoever the Lord their God shall command them**;
> **26** And they who keep their first estate shall be added upon; and they who keep not their first estate shall not have **glory** in

the same kingdom **with those** who keep their first estate; and **they** who keep their second estate shall **have glory added upon their heads** for ever and ever.

27 And **the Lord** said: Whom shall I send? And one answered like unto the Son of Man: Here am I, send me.

And another answered and said: Here am I, send me. And **the Lord** said: I will send **the first**."

And this…

(Moses 4:2 accents added)

"**2** But, behold, my Beloved Son, which was **my Beloved and Chosen from the beginning**, said unto me—Father, thy will be done, and **the glory** be thine forever."

Learning Points:
A. **Glory** will be added to the heads of those who keep the 2nd Estate, which is **this earth life**. It is all about the "Glory."
B. Also, Glory will be added to The Father through exalting more of his children.
C. **The Lord** in this pre-mortal existence scripture is God The Father. Not Jesus Christ. Jesus was the first volunteer to be the one to be sent to atone. This is evidence to show the word **"Lord"** can be applied to God The Father. Keep that in mind.
D. Lucifer was the 2nd volunteer. He was rejected and became the Devil.

The people who follow this path ultimately **add glory** to Father in Heaven. Thus, the Good Fruit is a person's completion of the path **to add additional glory** with God The Father.

3. What Did Jesus Say to The Children of Lehi?

After the destruction in the Americas around 33AD, Jesus visited the righteous Nephites and Lamanites (children of Lehi) at the temple in the Land of Bountiful.

This is a large section of scripture, so I will pick out the best parts on this topic, starting with **3rd Nephi 15:11 to 3rd Nephi 17:4**. (and to a semi-relevant extent **3rd Nephi 20:10 to 3rd Nephi 23:5**)

In this book, I don't have enough room to include these full 3rd Nephi writings. But, they are directly relevant and semi-relevant to The Prophecy of The Tame and Wild Olive Trees of Jacob 5. Please open your scriptures and read the section directly.

> (Selections of 3rd Nephi Chapter 15)
> "**11** And now it came to pass that when Jesus had spoken these words, he said **unto those twelve** whom he had chosen:
> **12** Ye are my disciples; and ye are a light unto this people, **who are a remnant of the house of Joseph.**
> **13** And behold, **this is the land of <u>your inheritance</u>**; and **<u>the Father</u>** hath given it unto you.

15 Neither at any time hath the Father given me commandment that I should tell unto them concerning **the other** tribes of the house of Israel, whom **the Father** hath **led away out of the land.**

19 But, verily, I say unto you that **the Father** hath commanded me, and I tell it unto you, that **ye were separated from among them** because of **their iniquity**; therefore it is **because of their iniquity that they know not of you.**
20 And verily, I say unto you again that **the other tribes** hath **the Father** separated from them; and it is **because of their iniquity that they know not of them.**"

Learning Points:
  A. The children of Lehi, who are of the House of Joseph have the Americas as their land of inheritance. It might not be quite that big. But, we know that a large portion of the current United States map is included.
  B. The Father **personally burned** the Northern 10 Tribes out from their lands in Northern Israel using the Assyrian invasion. This would represent burning the old dead branches. The Master/Lord of the Vineyard is the Father.
  C. Later, The Father **personally led** the remnant of the Lost 10 Tribes out of Assyria to their present location in the North. This would represent The Father **hiding** the young and tender branches in the nethermost parts of the vineyard.

D. It was because of iniquity (ie. the main tree's dying branches) that the Lost 10 Tribes became lost, only to the Jews and Christians in Jerusalem. The children of Lehi were told of their existence, but not of their exact location.
   a. The Jews in Jerusalem had several migrations in and out of their Promised Land; all by force of armies. However, not until the Romans attacked the Temple in 70AD did the Jews not come back to Jerusalem for about 1875 years.
   b. Yet, remember at this very same time 40AD-350AD...Christianity became prevalent through the Roman Empire. And was eventually enshrined into law as the state religion.
E. It was also because of the Jew's iniquity that they didn't know about the children of Lehi in the Americas. This matches perfectly to Jacob Chapter 5; because the last branch to be removed was the Jewish branch, along with their companions Benjamin and Levi. They didn't know where the other Lost 10 Tribes had gone. The Jewish branch of the tree was **burned** in 70 A.D. by the Roman General Titus, as he sacked Jerusalem. The remaining Jews were dispersed.

The scattering of the Remnant has happened. Both the Northern Kingdom of Israel and the Southern Kingdom of Judah are disbursed. **Next** comes the grafting-on of the wild branches of the Gentiles to the Church of Jesus Christ.

4. Jesus Continues the Sermon to The Children of Lehi As a Commandment Of The Father About The Gentiles

The sermon about these "other sheep" is expanded upon by the Savior. This single discourse spans over several chapters in 3rd Nephi.

> (Selections from 3rd Nephi Chapter 16)
> " **1** And verily, verily, I say unto you that **I have other sheep**, which are **not of this land, neither of the land of Jerusalem, neither in any parts of that land round about** whither I have been to minister."
>
> "**3** But I have received **a commandment of the Father** that I shall go unto them, and that they shall hear my voice, and shall be numbered among my sheep, that there may be one fold and one shepherd; therefore I go to show myself unto them.
> **4** And <u>**I command you that ye shall write these sayings**</u> after I am gone, that if it so be that my people at Jerusalem, they who have seen me and been with me in my ministry, do not ask the Father in my name, that they may receive a knowledge **of you** by the Holy Ghost, and also of **the other tribes** whom they know not of, that these sayings which ye shall write shall be kept and shall be **manifested unto the Gentiles**, that **through the fulness of the Gentiles**, the remnant of their seed, who shall be scattered forth upon the face of the earth because of their unbelief, may be brought in, or may be brought to a knowledge of me, their Redeemer."

Learning Points:
   A. The "other sheep" that the Savior is going to visit are The Lost 10 Tribes of Israel in the North. They are in a land. Their location is on earth in this vineyard.
   B. The commandment to show the Savior unto those Lost 10 Tribes comes directly from The Father. The Father is the Master/Lord of the Vineyard.
   C. The concepts in these scriptures are to come forth from the Gentiles who obtain The Book of Mormon in the last days. (ie. The Church of Jesus Christ of Latter-day Saints).
   D. This 1830 time period and beyond is called "the Fullness of the Gentiles". But not quite the "End of the Times of the Gentiles." **Keep that in mind.**

What Are The Times of the Gentiles

In the "last days," the Gentiles are to be the caretakers of the Church of Jesus Christ or **the tree trunk** itself. Including all the ordinances, direct revelation and priesthood; these are what make the Church function on the Earth.

It was once held by all of Israel. Then it was the Jews. Then the Times of The Gentiles was initiated.

Currently, in 2019 we live during the Times of The Gentiles.

It had its beginnings when Peter received the vision in Acts Chapter 10 about the unclean animals that he was to slay and eat. The baptism of the Roman Cornelius and all his family was next. **(See Appendix: Times of the Gentiles)**

I too am a Caucasian European by ancestry.

The Caucasian Europeans in the Church of Jesus Christ today should love that story of how Cornelius, **the first** Roman Gentile convert, joined the Church.

He paved the way for The Times of the Gentiles to be initiated by receiving an angel of God and acting upon what he was told.

However, "The Times of the Gentiles" will not always be open. There is a bumpy transition road ahead as The Times of the Gentiles are fulfilled, and the tree branches are adjusted, once more. **(See Appendix: Times of the Gentiles)**

SECTION 2: The NEW Gentile Converts Come Into The Church of Jesus Christ <u>And</u> Scattered Israel Is Flourishing At The Same Time

Original Artwork

5. Gentiles Begin to Produce Good Fruit

The work was finished. The wild Gentiles have been grafted into The Church of Jesus Christ. And the Israelite remnants have all been scattered to the furthest flung places of Earth's landmasses.

What happens next?

> (Jacob 5:15-18 accents added)
> "**15** And it came to pass that **a long time** passed away, and the Lord of the vineyard said unto his servant: Come, let **us go down** into the vineyard, that **we** may labor in the vineyard.
> **16** And it came to pass that the Lord of the vineyard, and also the servant, **went down** into the vineyard to labor. And it came to pass that the servant said unto his master: Behold, look here; behold the tree.
> **17** And it came to pass that the Lord of the vineyard looked and beheld the tree in the which the wild olive branches had been grafted; and it had sprung forth and **begun** to bear fruit. And he beheld that **it was good**; and **the fruit thereof was like unto the natural fruit**.
> **18** And he said unto the servant: Behold, the **branches of the wild tree have taken hold of the moisture of the root** thereof, that the **root thereof hath brought forth much strength**; and because of the much strength **of the root** thereof the **wild branches have brought forth tame fruit**. Now, if we had not grafted in these branches, the tree thereof would have perished. And now, behold, **I shall lay up much**

fruit, which the tree thereof hath brought forth; and the fruit thereof I shall lay up against the season, unto mine own self."

Original Artwork

Learning Points:

A. **A long time** passed away from the first scene to the 2nd scene. However, it appears that not much time passed compared to the next scene-jump, as we shall see.

    a. If the first scene is 745BC when the Northern 10 Tribes of Israel were taken captive into Assyria to around

40AD when the Gentiles **began** to be grafted into the church, then the time span is pretty wide.

    b. Also, if the 2nd scene opens when those same Gentiles that were grafted-in bear good fruit; yet before the great apostasy, then the 2nd scene opens about 45 to 200AD during the big influx of European Roman Gentiles into the Church of Jesus Christ, when Paul the apostle to the Gentiles was alive and preaching. (Paul died in Rome by the hands of Nero 64-68 A.D.). Note this 2nd scene could open as late as 200 A.D., after the Apostles deaths, but before the 2nd or 3rd generation of Gentile Christians have fully died out.

B. Let **us** go down – this shows that the Servant is **with** the Lord/Master. If the Vineyard is the landmasses on earth, then the Servant and Lord/Master are both not on the earth. They confer together to go down into the Vineyard. This is yet another evidence that The Servant is Jesus Christ and The Lord/Master is God the Father.

C. The original location of the Church of Jesus Christ with the Gentiles grafted-in had **began** to bear fruit. It was **not in full bloom** yet. The fruit was good, or the people's works were good at that point. Things looked promising for a **full harvest** using the Gentiles grafted into the church.

D. In this scene, the roots or scriptures + the teachings of God were the reason the Gentile branches succeeded in producing good fruit.

The good fruit of the NEW Christian Gentiles is flowing. But, how did those Gentiles come into the Church of Jesus Christ? What does it look like in real history?

6. Paul – The Apostle of The Gentiles

Was Paul the Apostle to the Gentiles? It appears that he thought he was. He mentioned it several times in the New Testament.

Also, it appears that Jesus planned for Saul/Paul to be sent to the Gentiles. That special message was given to Ananias; the brother that would heal Paul's eyes, and baptize Paul into the Church of Jesus Christ.

> (Acts 9:10-18 accents added)
> "**10** And there was a certain disciple at Damascus, named Ananias; and to him said the Lord in a vision, Ananias. And he said, Behold, I am here, Lord.
> **11** And the Lord said unto him, Arise, and go into the street which is called Straight, and inquire in the house of Judas for one called **Saul**, of Tarsus: for, behold, he prayeth,
> **12** And hath seen in a vision a man named Ananias coming in, and putting his hand on him, that he might receive his sight.
> **13** Then Ananias answered, Lord, I have heard by many of this man, how much evil he hath done to thy saints at Jerusalem:
> **14** And here he hath authority from the chief priests to bind all that call on thy name.
> **15** But the Lord said unto him, Go thy way: for he is a chosen vessel unto me, **to bear my name before the Gentiles**, and kings, and the children of Israel:

16 For I will shew him how great things he must suffer for my name's sake.

17 And Ananias went his way, and entered into the house; and **putting his hands on him** said, Brother Saul, the Lord, even Jesus, that appeared unto thee in the way as thou camest, hath sent me, that thou **mightest receive thy sight**, and be filled with the Holy Ghost.

18 And **immediately** there fell from his eyes as it had been scales: and **he received sight forthwith**, and arose, and was **baptized**."

Learning Points

A. Ananias healed Paul immediately of his blindness. And baptized him into the Church of Jesus Christ.
B. Paul's mission was to bear Jesus' name before **the Gentiles**, their kings, and to the children of Israel.
   a. This small prophecy came to pass in every way. Paul was an apostle sent to the Gentiles. He preached to the Romans. He preached to the Roman kings and governors several times from prison chains, and most likely to Caesar himself, although it is not recorded. Also, Paul preached to the Jews.
C. Paul did suffer greatly for Jesus' name.

Paul Also Read The Scriptures of The Old Testament Prophet Zenos

Apparently, at the time around 40-45 A.D., the Christians and Jews still had scriptures that we don't have in our current Old and New

Testaments. There are a variety of prophets that they refer to that we don't have today.

One of them was Zenos.

Zenos was never mentioned by name, but his content sure was.

In these next scriptures, Paul is comparing the **Jewish receptivity** /VS/ the **Gentile receptivity** to the Gospel.

Look and see what Paul understood about Zenos' *Prophecy of the Wild and Tame Olive Trees.*

Paul is writing to the NEW Gentile church members in Rome.

> (Romans 10:11-21 accents added)
> "**11** For the scripture saith, Whosoever believeth on him shall not be ashamed.
> **12** For there is **no difference between the Jew and the Greek**: for the same Lord over all is rich unto all that call upon him.
> **13** For whosoever shall call upon the name of the Lord shall be saved.
> **14** How then shall they call on him in whom they have not believed? and how shall they believe in him of whom they have not heard? and how shall they hear without **a preacher**?

15 And how shall they preach, except they **be sent**? as it is written, How beautiful are the feet of them that preach the gospel of peace, and bring glad tidings of good things!
16 But they have not all obeyed the gospel. For Esaias **[Isaiah]** saith, Lord, who hath believed our report?
17 So then **faith cometh by hearing**, and hearing by **the word of God.**
18 But I say, Have they not heard? Yes verily, their sound went into all the earth, and their words unto the ends of the world.
19 But I say, **Did not Israel know?** First Moses saith, <u>**I will provoke you to jealousy by them that are no people**</u>, and by <u>**a foolish nation**</u> I will anger you.
20 But Esaias **[Isaiah]** is very bold, and saith, <u>**I was found of them that sought me not**</u>; I was made manifest unto <u>**them that asked not after me.**</u>
21 But <u>**to Israel**</u> he saith, <u>**All day long I have stretched forth my hands unto a disobedient and gainsaying people.**</u>"

Learning Points

A. Jesus is not a respecter of persons. That is another way of saying that Jesus doesn't care what nationality we have ancestors from during this time period. Greeks were Gentiles.

B. **Faith comes by hearing or reading the word of God.** The preacher must be sent by one who has authority to send them.

C. In Isaiah, it states that Israel will be provoked to anger and jealousy **by the Gentiles**, as the Times of the Gentiles is beginning. (More on this Gentile connection to come.) The Jewish nation shall be offered The Messiah's Church but most will reject it. That is still true even today in 2019...however, their rejection of the Messiah **changes** at the end of the Battle of Armageddon.

God Always Preserves a Remnant of His People

The comparison of **Jewish receptivity** /VS/ **Gentile receptivity** to Christ's Church continues in Chapter 11 of Paul's writings to the Roman Saints.

This is where the fun begins.

> (Romans 11:1-6 accents added)
> "**1** I say then, Hath God cast away his people? God forbid. For **I also am an Israelite**, of the seed of Abraham, of the tribe of **Benjamin**.
> **2** God hath not cast away **his people** which he foreknew. Wot ye not what the scripture saith of Elias? how he maketh intercession to God against Israel, saying,
> **3** Lord, **they have killed thy prophets**, and **digged down thine altars**; and I am left alone, and they seek my life.
> **4** But what saith the answer of God unto him? I have reserved to myself **seven thousand men, who have not bowed the knee to the image of Baal.**
> **5** Even so then at this present time also **there is a remnant** according to the election of grace.
> **6** And if by grace, then is it no more of works: otherwise grace is no more grace. But if it be of works, then is it no more grace: otherwise work is no more work."

Learning Points
- A. Paul is an Israelite from the tribe of Benjamin. But, he is also a Roman citizen too. He has the best of both worlds.
- B. God has not cast away ALL of the Israelites. He saved a remnant.
- C. The Jewish Israelites have killed the prophets and have digged down the proper earth ramp alters of Israel and have erected altars to Baal, the Canaanite god of war and prosperity.

This Baal worship from the neighboring Canaanites was also the main reason that the Northern Kingdom of Israel was taken captive by the Assyrians and became lost to the world.

Idol worship of Baal, again was the original reason the Jews were taken captive into Babylon for a period.

God, the Master of the Vineyard didn't completely forsake his people then. And he won't now either. There shall be a remnant to be planted in other parts of the Vineyard.

The Jewish Israelite Stumblingblock That Eventually Provokes Jealousy of Another People

(continuing Romans 11:7-15 accents added)

7 What then? Israel hath not obtained that which he seeketh for; but **the election hath obtained it**, and the rest were **blinded**

8 (According as it is written, **God hath given them** the **spirit of slumber**, **eyes that they should not see**, and **ears that they should not hear**;) unto this day.

9 And David saith, Let **their table** be made **a snare**, and **a trap**, and a **stumblingblock**, and a recompence unto them:

10 Let **their eyes be darkened**, that they may not see, and bow down their back alway.

11 I say then, **Have they stumbled that they should fall**? God forbid: but rather **through their fall salvation is come unto the Gentiles**, for **to provoke them to jealousy**.

12 Now if the fall of them be the riches of the world, and **the diminishing of them the riches of the Gentiles**; how much more their fulness?

13 For **I speak to you Gentiles**, inasmuch as I am **the apostle of the Gentiles**, I magnify mine office:

14 If by any means I may provoke to emulation them which are my flesh, and might save some of them.

15 For if **the casting away** of them be the reconciling of the world, what shall **the receiving of them be**, but **life from the dead?"**

Learning Points
  A. The Jewish nation as a whole did not receive the true Church of The Messiah. Yet, some individual people that did receive it.
  B. The eyes and ears of Jewish Israelites have been "stopped" by God **on purpose**. So that the Gentiles will have an opportunity to be grafted into Israel. The feast meals of the table and animal sacrifice were their stumbling block to accepting the true church of the Messiah.
  C. The Israelites will be **provoked to jealousy** by <u>the Gentiles</u>. **There it is.** The group of people that will make the Jewish Israelites jealous…from the last chapter 10 material.
  D. Paul says he is the **apostle of the Gentiles**. And he intends to do that job very well.
  E. (v15) This "casting away" and "receiving" again phrasing. Paul is alluding that a remnant of the Jewish Israelites will be gathered back into the fold at a future date. It will be like a resurrection.

If A Group of <u>Natural</u> Branches Have Been Broken Off, The New <u>Wild</u> Branches Better Watch Out

In 40 A.D., at this time, the NEW Gentiles were being grafted onto the Church of God through the preaching of Paul the Apostle of the Gentiles. And those Gentile church members grew considerably. They even grew through the persecutions of the Roman state. The Times of the Gentiles had **begun**.

By 70 A.D. Rome had sacked Jerusalem, broken down the temple, and killed a great percentage of Jews. The rest were scattered throughout Europe for millennia.

But, there will come a moment in the future when the Times of the Gentiles **is fulfilled and comes to an end.** As shown in this Prophecy of The Tame and Wild Olive Trees. And **Paul had read it too**.

> (continuing Romans 11:16-24 accents added)
> "**16** For if the firstfruit be holy, the lump is also holy: and if the root be holy, **so are the branches**.
> **17** And if **some** of the **branches be broken off**, and **thou, being a wild olive tree**, wert **grafted in among them**, and with them **partakest of the root and fatness of the olive tree**;
> **18 Boast not against the branches**. But if thou boast, thou bearest not the root, but the root thee.
> **19** Thou wilt say then, **The branches were broken off, that I might be grafted in.**
> **20** Well; because of unbelief they were broken off, and thou standest by faith. **Be not highminded, but fear**:
> **21** For **if God spared not the natural branches**, take heed lest he **also spare not thee**.
> **22** Behold therefore the goodness and severity of God: on **them which fell, severity**; but **toward thee, goodness**, if thou continue in his goodness: otherwise **thou also shalt be cut off**.
> **23** And they also, if they abide **not still in unbelief, shall be grafted in**: for God is able **to graft them in again**.

24 For if **thou** wert cut out of the **olive tree** which is **wild** by **nature**, and wert **grafted contrary to nature into a good olive tree**: how much more shall **these,** which be the **natural branches**, be grafted into **their own olive tree**?"

Learning Points

A. Paul had seen and considered the Old Testament prophet Zenos as **authoritative**. Paul also used the prophecy to teach the NEW Gentile converts **at Rome** about their future.
B. **The roots = the scriptures as the Word of God, first recorded by living prophets.** Paul understood that the roots of the olive tree were **the most important part**.
C. Israel as it connects to the root through the branches, becomes holy as well.
D. The Jewish Israelites were broken off. And the Gentiles were grafted into the tree and connected to the good roots.
E. For the Believing Gentiles to boast against the natural-born Israelites is not good. Because the European Gentiles day will end, because of unbelief, just as the Israelites did. That will be the end of the Times of the Gentiles.

I find this material amazing. That sitting in our New Testament scriptures is Paul preaching to the Gentile Christian converts of Rome about Zenos' Prophecy of The Tame and Wild Olive Trees.

But, wait...there is more.

The Future Deliverer of Natural Born Israel

Israel has needed a Deliverer from time to time. And this "last-days" time period is no different. It was **a covenant promise** by God given to Israel as their branches were being broken off around 40 A.D. See below.

> (continuing Romans 11:25-36 accents added)
> "**25** For I would not, brethren, that ye should be **ignorant of this mystery**, lest ye should be wise in your own conceits; that blindness in part is happened to Israel, **until the fulness of the Gentiles be come in.**
> **26** And so **all Israel** shall be saved: as it is written, There shall come out of **Sion the Deliverer**, and **shall turn away ungodliness from Jacob**:
> **27** For **this is my covenant unto them**, **when** I shall take away their sins.
> **28** As concerning the gospel, **they are enemies** for your sakes: but as touching the election, **they are beloved** for the fathers' sakes.
> **29** For the gifts and calling of God are without repentance.
> **30** For as **ye** in times past **have not believed God**, yet have **now** obtained mercy through **their** unbelief:
> **31** Even so have **these** also **now not believed**, that through **your mercy** they also may obtain mercy.
> **32** For God hath concluded them all in unbelief, that he might have mercy upon all.

33 O the depth of the riches both of the wisdom and knowledge of God! how unsearchable are his judgments, and his ways past finding out!

34 For who hath known the mind of the Lord? or who hath been his counsellor?

35 Or who hath first given to him, and it shall be recompensed unto him again?

36 For of him, and through him, and to him, are all things: to whom be glory for ever. Amen."

Learning Points

A. The **mystery** that Paul was considering was how Israel would one day be **re-attached** back onto the Olive Tree. And he wasn't just considering the Jewish Israelites, but **all** of the 12 Tribes of Israel.

B. **When** shall this happen? When "the fullness of the Gentiles be come in." After the Times of the Gentiles is completed. In 2019, we are still living **during** this Times of the Gentiles. (See: *The "Last Days" Timeline – Volume 1* by James T. Prout to know when that happens in the future)

C. **The Deliverer shall come out of Sion (Zion)** – In the future, there shall be a strong Deliverer of Israel. One very good candidate for this particular Deliverer is John the Beloved Revelator who will be at the front of the Lion Kingdom of the Lost 10 Tribes of Israel, when they take down the remaining forces of the 4th Beast Kingdom of The Gentiles in America and beyond. However, John is not the only Deliverer of Israel in the future to 2019. There are others. (See: *The Last Days Timeline*

– *Volume 1* appendix item *The Root, The Stem, The Branch, and The Rod, All of Jessie*)
- D. The **covenant promise** that this **Deliverer** would come was known and expected all the way back in 40 A.D. at **the start** of the Times of the Gentiles.
- E. Paul understood that through Israel's fall and removal from the Church of God, the Gentiles would now have it. However, he also noted that in the future, The Gentiles would fall, and Israel would be re-grafted back into the Church of God. That all peoples may obtain mercy. Paul glories in God that this was a very wise plan.

Paul had read Zenos's writings. Which means that Zenos' writings were still available and around at 40 A.D.

From what I understand, the Jews had **cast out** Zenos' writings, because they said some rather unsavory things. But, then so did Zenos directly as a prophet of God. (See appendix: Teachings of Zenos)

However, if the Christians in Rome had read this prophecy and were instructed in it by Paul by letter, it seems plausible that they would have resurrected the old Zenos book and read it a bit more.

If that be the case, what happened to Zenos' book within the new Christian church? Why don't we find any evidence for it today?

It is a wonder that we have Zenos' teachings at all. Knowledge of Zenos had to be restored through The Book of Mormon with the prophet Joseph Smith Jr.

7. What Happens to The NEW Gentile Christians After Paul is Martyred?

The NEW Gentile Christians of the Roman Empire are bearing fruit. Good fruit, **like** unto the natural fruit.

In history, this is the golden age when Christianity was spreading under the Apostles to just a few generations afterward.

But then, the persecution began.

The Roman Persecution Period

State persecution ramped up starting in 64 A.D. under Nero with the Great Fire of Rome being blamed on the Christians.
(See https://en.wikipedia.org/wiki/Persecution_of_Christians_in_the_Roman_Empire)

Paul, the apostle to the Gentiles, was believed to have been killed by Nero in Rome.

Nero's Torches (Christian Candlesticks) (Wikipedia - Public Domain)

This was the same period when Christians were being fed to lions in the Roman Coliseum. They would rather **suffer martyrdom** than to perform sacrifices to the Roman gods of the state-mandated religion.

Yet, during this same time period 64 A.D. to around 250 A.D. the church was flourishing with many many new members. So many new members in fact that with the 313 A.D. Edict of Milan, the persecution of Christians ceased.

By the time Constantine ruled in 324 A.D., and soon after…The new state church of Rome would become Christ-based. Constantine declared himself supreme ruler of the NEW state religion of Rome.

The 3 best sources of information on this topic include:
1. *The Great Apostasy* by James Talmadge – Download the free audiobook here:
   https://www.lastdaystimeline.com/great-apostasy
2. *History of the Early Christian Church* by Cheetham – Available here: https://www.lastdaystimeline.com/free-audiobooks
3. *Foxes Book of the Martyrs by John Fox* – Download the free audiobook here:
   https://www.lastdaystimeline.com/foxes-book-of-martyrs

What Happened to These Christian Martyrs?

Fortunately, we know what happened to them. These martyred men and women lived during the early parts of the 5th Seal of John the Revelator.

They are seen praising God in white robes. The government persecution of Christians was not done yet. There would be more.

> (Revelation: 6:9-11 accents added)
> "**9** And when he had **opened** the **fifth seal**, I saw under the altar the souls of them that **were slain for the word of God**, and for the testimony which they held:
> **10** And they cried with a loud voice, saying, How long, O Lord, holy and true, dost thou not judge and avenge our blood on them that dwell on the earth?

11 And **white robes** were given unto every one of them; and it was said unto them, that they should rest yet for **a little season**, until **their fellowservants** also and their brethren, that **should be killed as they were, should be fulfilled**."

Learning Points:

A. At the **beginning of the 5th Seal**, at the time of Jesus' mortal ministry, there were martyrs for the word of God and for the testimony of Jesus Christ which they held. They were Christians.

B. They were preserved, upheld and given white robes for their faithfulness.

C. Yet, there were more Christian martyrs to come upon the Earth. However, **not in the 5th Seal**, but in a future Seal. It turns out later in the Book of Revelation to be the **end of the 6th Seal**. Those Christians that would not bow to **the 4th Beast Kingdom of the Gentiles**. (which is yet future to 2019) This period of the future, will be called the **Great Persecution Period**. (See: *The Last Days Timeline – Volume 1* for details on what this looks like.)

The NEWLY grafted Christian Gentiles are growing well in the Church of Jesus Christ. But what about the other trees in the vineyard? How are they doing at 33-200 A.D.?

8. What Do The Lost 10 Tribes Look Like At 33-200 A.D.?

The Lord/Master now takes a tour of the vineyard with The Servant and displays the Lost 10 Tribes in the nethermost regions of the Earth's landmasses.

Remember a few things. The Lost 10 Tribes were taken **to** the North. Also, they return **from** the icy North. Further, in 33-200 A.D., they are **still living in The Vineyard**.

In the next few verses, look at the types of land that is available in the North.

> (Jacob 5:19-22 accents added)
> "**19** And it came to pass that the Lord of the vineyard said unto the servant: Come, let us go to **the nethermost part of the vineyard**, and behold if **the natural branches** of the tree have not brought forth much fruit also, that I may lay up of the fruit thereof against the season, unto mine own self.
> **20** And it came to pass that they went forth **whither the master had hid** the natural branches of the tree, and he said unto the servant: Behold **these**; and he beheld **the first** that it had brought forth much fruit; and he beheld also that **it was good**. And he said unto the servant: Take of the fruit thereof, and lay it up against the season, that I may preserve it unto mine own self; for behold, said he, this long time have **I** nourished it, and it hath brought forth much fruit.

21 And it came to pass that **the servant said unto his master: How comest thou hither to plant this tree, or this branch of the tree**? For behold, it was **the poorest spot** in all the land of thy vineyard.

22 And the Lord of the vineyard said unto him: **Counsel me not**; I knew that it was a poor spot of ground; wherefore, I said unto thee, **I have nourished it** this long time, and thou beholdest that it hath brought forth much fruit."

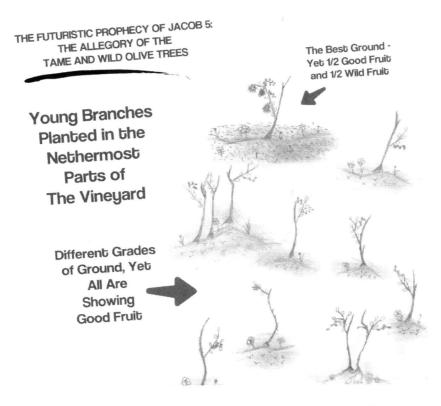

Original Artwork

Learning Points:

A. The Master/Lord invites the Servant to go down into the furthest parts of the vineyard on a tour. At this point, the Servant doesn't know where the Master/Lord planted those natural branches of Israel. This information was specifically hidden from the Servant.

B. **Branch #1** – As shown later in this sequence of verses, these branches nearly represent the exact order that the Tribes of

Israel were born in. If correct, this first branch represents the Tribe of Rueben.

1. Apparently, Rueben was planted in "the poorest spot" in all the vineyard. So, wherever the Tribe of Rueben is located today, that ground location doesn't seem very good.
NOTE: There is one more tribe that was planted in a worse spot of ground.
    i. Remember: the land locations in this vineyard of Earth would include the Sahara Desert, Antarctica, Mongolia, Australia's inner land mass, Russia's Siberia, Northern Alaska/Canada, and Greenland. Those represent some pretty tough parts on the Earth to live. However, humans have found ways to tame even these hard places.
    ii. Note that these poor spots of ground are still in this vineyard. The master did **not** plant these tribes of Israel **in another vineyard**.
        1. **Author's Analysis:** I have read some authors that claim that the 10 Lost Tribes have left this earth and are on another planet or lobe of this planet that reside somewhere else in space. This prophecy doesn't show that. This is another evidence point to show that The Lost 10 Tribes are still located on this Earth, in this Vineyard. (Note: understanding the mechanism of the 10 Lost Tribes being

hidden is less important than understanding that **they are apart**.)
   2. The fruit of Rueben was good. Even for such a bad spot of ground.
   3. **Author's Analysis**: I've heard it said by other people that these branches are in the birth order of the sons of Jacob/Israel. The idea comes from the "last" being a description of Joseph's sons Ephraim and Manasseh. With the children of Lehi being their descendants. The problem with this model is that the very last son of Jacob/Israel was Benjamin, not Joseph. The model is close, but doesn't perfectly fit.
      i. **But:** Since Benjamin stayed with Judah in the Palestine area when the Northern 10 Tribes became lost, Benjamin was not relocated until later with Judah in 70AD. Thus, the youngest tribe to be relocated early was Joseph. So from a birth order model, it only partly fits. But, from an actual tribe removal model, it fits better. Just as it should.
C. The Servant inquires of the Master/Lord as to why he chose this bad spot of ground. The Master/Lord wanted to demonstrate how well the natural branches were doing through his own labor. Not the labor of the Servant. It appears The Father was working directly with The Lost 10 Tribes of Israel, to this point in history 33-60AD. Not Jesus.
   1. Also, as shown above, this was the approximate time in history 33-34 AD that Jesus received a commandment

from The Father to visit the children of Lehi in the Americas and the Lost 10 Tribes of Israel. Spot on.

The Tribes of Israel in normal birth order are:
1. Reuben
2. Simeon
3. Levi
4. Judah
5. Dan
6. Naphtali
7. Gad
8. Asher
9. Issachar
10. Zebulun
11. Joseph
    a. Manasseh
    b. Ephraim
12. Benjamin

Some websites list the order a little differently according to other sections of scripture. However, this is the normal birth order.

Where is Simeon and Levi, the 2nd and 3rd Tribe of Israel?

(Jacob 5:23-24 accents added)

"**23** And it came to pass that the Lord of the vineyard said unto his servant: Look hither; behold **I** have planted **another branch of the tree** also; and thou knowest that **this spot of ground was poorer than the first**. But, behold the tree. **I** have nourished it this long time, and it hath brought forth **much fruit; therefore, gather it**, and lay it up against the season, that I may preserve it unto mine own self.

24 And it came to pass that the Lord of the vineyard said again unto his servant: Look hither, and behold **another branch also**, which I have planted; behold that **I have nourished it** also, and it hath brought **forth fruit**."

Learning Points:

A. **Branch #2** – The Master/Lord of the vineyard is demonstrating the success of the 2nd branch to The Servant. The Servant didn't know where The Master/Lord hid it.
   1. This 2nd Branch would represent the Tribe of Simeon. The 2nd born son of Jacob/Israel.
   2. The ground location is even worse than the first.
B. The Master/Lord himself nourished this Tribe of Israel himself. Again, The Father cared for the Lost 10 Tribes personally. Not Jesus, until this point in the Timeline 33-34AD.
C. The Tribe of Simeon did bring forth much good fruit.
D. Notice the commandment of The Master/Lord to The Servant to gather the fruit and preserve it. This is exactly Jesus' role in the Plan of Salvation. The Servant represents Jesus Christ.
E. **Branch #3** – The 3rd branch represents the Tribe of Levi or Dan. Because **the Tribe of Levi, being temple workers**, may have stayed in Judah with the Temple when the Lost 10 Tribes were carried away by Assyria in 721BC. Also, this 3rd branch can't be Judah which is the 4th son. So, either Levi (#3) or Dan (#5).

1. This tribe also brought forth much good fruit.
2. The Master/Lord also personally nourished Levi/Dan.
3. Notice there is no mention of the bad or good ground with this branch #3.

Where Was the Tribe of Joseph Living in 33-34 A.D.?

(Jacob 5:25-28 accents added)

"**25** And he said unto the servant: Look hither and **behold the last**. Behold, this have I planted in a **good spot of ground**; and I have nourished it this long time, and **only a part of the tree hath brought forth tame fruit**, and the **other part of the tree hath brought forth wild fruit**; behold, I have nourished this tree like unto the others.

26 And it came to pass that the Lord of the vineyard said unto the servant: **Pluck off the branches that have not brought forth good fruit, and cast them into the fire.**

27 But behold, **the servant said** unto him: Let us prune it, and dig about it, and **nourish it a little longer**, that **perhaps** it may bring forth good fruit unto thee, that thou canst lay it up against the season.

28 And it came to pass that **the Lord** of the vineyard **and the servant** of the Lord of the vineyard **did nourish all** the fruit of the vineyard."

Learning Points:

A. **Last Branch** – This last branch was not noted by a number. Just that it was "last". This last branch represents the Tribe of Joseph. Zenos receives details about the seed of Joseph.

These few verses are probably why Jacob, a son of Lehi (Through Manasseh) is reading this to his people. This describes the children of Lehi's plight in their future.

    a. Remember: the people of Nephi through their 1000 years of history have these tribes: Manasseh, Ephraim through Ishmael's family, and Judah through the People of Zarahemla. To say that there are only 2 divisions of the children of Lehi (Nephites and Lamanites) as the only Tribe of Israel represented on this Last Branch is not entirely accurate. So things are not perfect along the lines of this prophecy. But, they are generally correct.

    b. **The Tame/Good Fruit on the Last Branch** = the Nephites/righteous Lamanites.

    c. **The Wild/Bad Fruit on the Last Branch** = the wicked Lamanites/Nephite dissenters. Note: This is **the first time** in all the vineyard that we encounter Wild/Bad Fruit.

B. Notice the command of The Master/Lord – cut off the wicked parts and burn them. Yet, the loving Servant asks for more time to turn these wicked parts around. The plan was adopted, because all the trees of the vineyard received nourishment. **No burning of branches in this round of the 33 A.D. Vineyard Check**. The Servant acted as a **Mediator**.

    a. That plan doesn't work out very well, as we shall see.

The Lost 10 Tribes and Nephites have started to produce some young good fruit. But, how did they get their roots started, when only a branch was cut off?

How were they made to flourish with deep roots?

The next chapter holds the answer of **how simple branches grow deep roots**.

9. The 33 A.D. Visit of Jesus To Work With The Lost 10 Tribes And Have Them Record His Words as Scripture To Deepen Their Root Systems

The time that Jesus **first** visits the Lost 10 Tribes is just after visiting with the Nephites in 33 A.D. Up to that point, Jesus had never seen them. The Master/Father was the only one that knew where He put them.

Now it was time for Jesus, their long-awaited Messiah to visit and talk with them. **His word** to them would be included in their scriptural roots.

One day we will have those scriptural Roots to add to our own.

(Note: these **first 4** verses below were used in a previous chapter. However, this time we **will continue** the narrative that Jesus spoke to **deepen the root systems** of these branches of Israel.)

> (3rd Nephi 16:1-4 accents added)
> "**1** And verily, verily, I say unto you that **I have other sheep**, which are not of this land, neither of the land of Jerusalem, neither in any parts of that land round about whither I have been to minister.
> **2** For they of whom I speak are they **who have not as yet heard my voice**; **neither have I at any time** manifested myself unto them.

3 But I have received **a commandment of the Father** that I shall go unto them, and that **they shall hear my voice**, and **shall be** numbered among **my sheep**, that there may be one fold and one shepherd; therefore I go to show myself unto them.

4 And I command you that **ye shall write** these sayings after I am gone, that if it so be that my people at Jerusalem, they who have seen me and been with me in my ministry, do not ask the Father in my name, that they may receive a knowledge of you by the Holy Ghost, and also of **the other tribes** whom they know not of, that **these sayings which ye shall write** shall be kept and shall be manifested unto **the Gentiles**, that through **the fulness of the Gentiles**, the remnant of their seed, who shall be scattered forth upon the face of the earth because of their unbelief, may be brought in, or may be brought to a knowledge of me, their Redeemer."

Learning Points:

A. It appears that Jesus is saying that He had not at any time **seen nor spoken** with these Lost 10 Tribes from 721 B.C. until 33 A.D. just after he visited the Nephites. Remember it was The Master/Father who hid them whithersoever **He** will. The Servant didn't know where they were. As to **why** Heavenly Father hid that knowledge from Jesus Christ, I know not and I won't venture. I do know that The Father also doesn't tell The Son everything. Like the specific time of **Jesus' own** 2nd coming. If you have a plausible idea in this area, contact me at www.LastDaysTimeline.com

B. The Father gave Jesus a commandment to visit and tend to these transplanted Natural Branches of the main Olive Tree.
C. The writings of the Nephites and the other Tribes of Israel that Jesus visits are commanded **to write** what he says. This written text becomes scripture to them. This is how scripture is originally made.
D. The **last-days Believing Gentiles** shall receive these writings in the future and be grafted into Israel. Just as the next few verses show.
E. Only **after** the *Fullness of the Gentiles* are the Lost Tribes gathered.

The "Last Days" Believing Gentiles /VS/ UnBelieving Gentiles

A little further down the timeline comes this next section of scripture. It was important to the overall timeline of events that Jesus was directly speaking about, so I've included it here. It is a little more forward-looking than 33 A.D.

This next scripture shows 2 last days Gentile groups.

> (3rd Nephi 16:5-13 accents added)
> "**5** And **then will I gather them** in from the four quarters of the earth; and **then will I fulfil the covenant which the Father hath made unto all the people of the house of Israel**.
> **6** And blessed are **the Gentiles, because of their belief in me**, in and of the Holy Ghost, which witnesses unto them of me and of the Father.

7 Behold, because of **their belief in me**, saith the Father, and because of **the unbelief of you, O house of Israel**, in **the latter day** shall **the truth come unto the Gentiles**, that the fulness of these things shall be made known unto them.

8 But wo, saith the Father, unto the **unbelieving of the Gentiles**—for notwithstanding **they have come forth upon the face of this land**, and have scattered my people who are of the house of Israel; and my people who are of the house of Israel have been cast out from among them, and have been trodden under feet by them;

9 And because of **the mercies of the Father unto the Gentiles**, and also **the judgments of the Father upon my people who are of the house of Israel**, verily, verily, I say unto you, that after all this, and I have caused my people who are of the house of Israel to be smitten, and to be afflicted, and to be slain, and to be cast out from among them, and to become hated by them, and to become a hiss and a byword among them—

10 And thus commandeth the Father that I should say unto you: **At that day when** the **Gentiles shall sin against my gospel**, and shall **reject the fulness of my gospel**, and shall be lifted up in the pride of their hearts **above all nations**, and above all the people of the whole earth, and shall be filled with all manner of lyings, and of deceits, and of mischiefs, and all manner of hypocrisy, and murders, and **priestcrafts**, and whoredoms, and of **secret abominations**; and if they shall do all those things, **and shall reject the fulness of my gospel**, behold, saith the Father, **I will bring the fulness of my gospel from among them.**

11 And **then** will I remember my covenant which I have made unto my people, O house of Israel, and **I will bring my gospel unto them.**

12 And I will show unto thee, O house of Israel, that **the Gentiles shall not have power over you**; but I will remember my covenant unto you, O house of Israel, and ye shall come unto the knowledge of the fulness of my gospel.

13 But **if** the Gentiles will repent and return unto me, saith the Father, behold **they shall be numbered among my people, O house of Israel.**"

Learning Points:
   A. **After** the **Believing Gentiles** receive The Book of Mormon, and the *Fullness* of the Gentiles has happened, then the covenant of the Father to the 12 Tribes of Israel will commence. They will get their promised lands back.
   B. Those lands shall be taken from the **Unbelieving Gentiles** that persecuted Israel.
   C. **Bad Fruit** = This list of negative qualities for the Gentiles' sins on the Promised Land include; lots of **priestcrafts** and **secret combinations**. Plus the normal run-of-the-mill sins. These in total represent the Bad Wild Fruit of The Prophecy of The Tame and Wild Olive Trees. **Jesus himself defined it.**
   D. The trigger point for the end of the *Times of the Gentiles* is **when they actively fight against and reject the fullness of the Gospel of the Lamb**. Which at that point…is held by the Believing Gentiles. (Think about that. This **future to 2019** time period is called *The Great Persecution Period*. It takes place

toward the middle-end of the 4th Beast Kingdom of the Gentiles.)

E. The Believing Gentiles shall be numbered among Jesus' people of Israel. This is through baptism and confirmation into The Church of Jesus Christ of Latter-day Saints and taking upon themselves the covenant with Abraham. Adopted as his seed.

*Very Important Point - For you to know about these **two last days Gentile groups** is most profound. This **one scriptural concept** can keep you from being led astray.

The Lord Jesus Christ has just stated: **There are <u>Believing Gentiles</u> and <u>Unbelieving Gentiles</u>**.

We have seen that the **Believing Gentiles** are adopted into the House of Israel.

Follow the prophet and "Stay in the Old Ship Zion."

All Is Looking Good in The Vineyard Right Now in 33 A.D. to 200 A.D. – It is On Track

The early fruit of the new Gentiles is doing well. The short-lived Law of Consecration and massive Gentile growth is on-track.

The Lost 10 Tribes are also doing well with their fruit.

The Nephites' fruit in the America's is looking good too. As this is the "People of God" period where they are also practicing the Law of Consecration.

All is looking promising in the Vineyard from 33 A.D. to 200 A.D.

Then **a long time passes away**, before the next venture through the Vineyard.

Something very unexpected happens.

SECTION 3: The Gentile's Great Apostasy Along With Israel's Great Apostasy At The Same Time – No Good Fruit

Original Artwork

10. What Happens After The Gentile's Great Apostasy? How Does The Master/Lord Want to Deal With This Problem?

After the 60-200AD visit, when the new Gentile fruit was doing good. And the Lost Tribes of Israel's fruit was doing well and on target to reach maximum production.

Then something went wrong.

Very wrong.

It appears that the Master and the Servant were both **surprised** to see how bad things got in the Vineyard upon their next inspection.

What happened to the Gentiles and the other Lost Tribes of Israel to cause such a disaster?

> (Jacob 5:29-32 accents added)
> "**29** And it came to pass that **a long time** had passed away, and the Lord of the vineyard said unto his servant: Come, **let us go down into the vineyard**, that <u>we</u> may labor <u>again</u> in the vineyard. For behold, the time draweth near, and **the end soon cometh**; wherefore, I must lay up fruit against the season, unto mine own self.
> **30** And it came to pass that the Lord of the vineyard and the servant went down into the vineyard; and they came to the tree

whose natural branches had been broken off, and the wild branches had been grafted in; and behold **all sorts of fruit** did cumber the tree.

31 And it came to pass that the Lord of the vineyard **did taste** of the fruit, **every sort** according to its number. And the Lord of the vineyard said: Behold, this long time have we nourished this tree, and **I have laid up unto myself against the season <u>much fruit</u>**.

32 But behold, **this time** it hath brought forth **much fruit**, and there is **<u>none of it which is good</u>**. And behold, there are **<u>all kinds of bad fruit</u>**; and it profiteth me nothing, notwithstanding all our labor; and now it grieveth me that I should lose this tree."

Original Artwork

Learning Points:

A. A long time passed away – from the rest of this passage, the timeline point of this event where the Master/Lord Father and The Servant/Jesus check on the Vineyard again, would be the year **1820 as Joseph Smith sees The Father and The Son in The First Vision.** They **both came down together** to labor in the Vineyard. So, the rest of the description is a time when The Church of Jesus Christ is NOT on the Earth, but about to be restored.

B. Let Us Go Down – This is a joint work effort between the Father and Son

C. The End Soon Cometh – In the history of the world 1820 A.D., would represent a time near the end. It is well after the ½ way-point in this Earth's existence, including the 1000 year Millennium.

D. On the main tree, that the Gentiles had been grafted, all sorts of fruit did happen on the same branches of the Gentiles. **Not one single bad fruit.** But, **many varieties** of bad fruits. This is indicative of a time period that is after the General Apostasy of the Gentiles; way after. If this scene was taken in 1200 A.D., there would not be **multiple varieties** of Bad Fruit. No. This had **lots of types** of bad fruit. Indicative that the now Bad Gentile Fruit, at this moment in 1820, has many different belief systems that were formed in the Gentile Branches and profiteth the Master/Lord/Father nothing. No glory. The General Apostasy happened first. Then the Gentiles had multiplied into **dozens of different organized belief systems** by 1820.

   a. (Note: Keeping the definitions straight in the mind is important. **The fruit is the byproduct of the branches**. More on this topic of the Gentile branches that overrun the doctrinal roots to come.) (See: Appendix – Recognizing The Great Apostasy)

E. The Master/Lord had laid up much good fruit from these Gentile branches in the past. But, not this time. Something is different.

F. The Master/Lord just to make sure, **taste-tested each type** of bad fruit, just to make sure it was bad.

Why Did The Gentiles Go Astray into Apostasy in the First Place?

In 1820 A.D., there were lots of organized denominations. Some in Europe; some in America; and some all over the world. Why are there so many denominations?

Does Father want so many different belief systems? Does Jesus claim them all as his own, as some people profess?

In this Old Testament prophecy of Zenos, recorded in The Book of Mormon, that question is answered. This situation is distressing to The Father and The Son. So much so, that The Father concluded to **burn it all**. But, the Son acted on our behalf as Mediator once again.

> (Jacob 5:33-37 accents added)
> "**33** And the Lord of the vineyard said unto the servant: What shall we do unto the tree, that I may preserve again good fruit thereof unto mine own self?
> **34** And the servant said unto his master: Behold, because thou didst graft in the branches of the wild olive tree **they have nourished the roots**, that **they are alive** and they have not perished; wherefore thou beholdest that **they are yet good**.
> **35** And it came to pass that the Lord of the vineyard said unto his servant: The tree profiteth me nothing, and **the roots**

thereof profit me nothing so long as it shall bring forth evil fruit.

36 Nevertheless, I know that **the roots are good**, and for mine own purpose I have preserved them; and because of **their much strength they have hitherto brought forth, from the wild branches, good fruit.**

37 But behold, the **wild branches have grown and have overrun the roots thereof**; and **because** that the wild branches have overcome the roots thereof it hath brought forth much evil fruit; and **because** that it hath brought forth so much evil fruit thou beholdest that **it beginneth to perish**; and it will **soon become ripened**, that it may be **cast into the fire**, except we should **do something** for it to preserve it."

Learning Points:

A. The Gentiles brought fourth many types of evil fruit. But, **they have kept alive the roots/scriptures/words of God, in general**. The **roots were kept alive** through the **early** Gentile's actions.

   1. The actions of the **early** Gentiles keep the roots alive. This is recorded in 1st Nephi 13:20-23. (See it there)
   2. We see in 2nd Nephi 28 and 29 that the **later** Gentile branches did indeed bring forth all types of bad doctrines using the same Bible. Those doctrines did **overrun the root scriptures**. The creeds and doctrines of men have produced the Bad Fruit, as a byproduct. (Stay tuned, Jesus specifically defines **the Gentile Bad Fruit** soon.)

1. This is why we believe the Bible is the word of God, as far as it is translated correctly. (See: Appendix 2: Recognizing The Great Apostasy)
B. In the past 33-70 A.D., the strong roots helped the Gentiles to bring forth good fruit.
C. But now 1820 A.D., the Gentile branches have taken doctrine unto themselves and have **overrun the scriptures** and the doctrines taught therein. The Bad Fruit is a natural byproduct of this scenario.
D. The altered Gentile belief systems were killing the tree and the good roots. The whole tree was beginning to die. The various bad fruit types were ripening into maturity in 1820. Soon, if The Father and The Son didn't do something drastic, the whole tree including the good roots would need to be burned.

For all the Gentiles wild branches to have produced bad fruit, after having good fruit early on, something must have taken place that went from good to bad.

Somewhere they must have stumbled. Let's see if **the special book compiled for our day** has the answers.

11. What Is The Future Gentile's Stumbling Block That Nephi Saw in 600 B.C.?

(public domain)

Nephi was a great prophet.

This son of Lehi did all that his father asked of him.

He even received his own revelations direct from the Almighty.

In the longest prophetic revelation that Nephi recorded, he received a plethora of detailed information about the future. Materials that were just for his people and materials for the future Gentiles that would inhabit the promised land.

These chapters range from 1 Nephi Chapters 11 – 14. Then Nephi uses the rest of his 2 books in explaining the concepts that he saw in this vision of the future. Including the Isaiah chapters.

There is a LOT of material here concerning the last days. However, we want to focus our attention on the stumbling block that the Gentiles have, that are upon the promised land.

Who Put The Stumbling Block In Front of The Gentiles?

To see this stumbling block in action, let's start at the beginning:

> (1 Nephi 13:24-26, accents added)
> "**24** And the angel of the Lord said unto me: Thou hast beheld that **the book** proceeded forth from the mouth of a Jew; and **when** it proceeded forth from the mouth of a Jew it contained **the fulness** of the gospel of the Lord, of whom the twelve Apostles bear record, and they bear record according to the truth which is in the Lamb of God.
> **25** Wherefore, these things go forth **from the Jews in purity unto the Gentiles**, according to the truth which is in God.

(public image)

26 And **after** they go forth by the hand of the twelve Apostles of the Lamb, **from the Jews unto the Gentiles**, thou seest the formation of that great and abominable church, which is most abominable above all other churches; for behold, **they have taken away from the gospel of the Lamb many parts which are plain and most precious; and also many covenants of the Lord** have they taken away."

Learning Points:
  A. For a quick analysis, The Great and Abominable Church took away many plain and precious parts of the gospel out of the belief system and out of the book of the religion, namely the Holy Bible. Including many covenants, which are specifically mentioned.
  B. It wasn't just a change in doctrine, but a change in ordinances that include covenant agreements with God.

What Is The Stumbling Block Itself?

Now, I didn't see the stumbling block in those scriptures, so let's discover it.

(1 Nephi 13:29, accents added)
"29 And **after** these plain and precious things were taken away it goeth forth unto all the nations of the Gentiles; and **after** it goeth forth unto all the nations of the Gentiles, yea, even **across the many waters** which thou hast seen with the Gentiles which have gone forth out of captivity, thou seest—because of the many plain and precious things which have been taken out of the book, which **were** plain unto the

understanding of the children of men, according to the plainness which is in the Lamb of God—**because of these things which are taken away out of the gospel of the Lamb, an exceedingly great many <u>do stumble</u>**, yea, insomuch that Satan hath great power over them."

Learning Points:
A. The Stumbling Block itself is the lack of scripture that was purposefully taken out of the cannon of The Holy Bible and the adjustments to the ordinances of the true religion of The Lamb.
B. Notice the time element of ***when***…after the special book has traveled with the Gentiles "across the many waters" to the Americas. That puts the date around the 1600's and 1700's. By 1820, it was complete.

What Does The Stumbling Block Look Like in Modern Times?

In verse 32, the condition the Gentiles have is considered "blindness." In verse 34, the stumbling block is reconfirmed again as the lack of information caused by The Mother of Harlots.

However, we don't see the main topics of religious confusion until we read the explanation of Nephi's revelation as he is explaining the Isaiah chapters. The explanation is recorded in 2nd Nephi chapters 26-33. It starts after the Isaiah insertions.

(2 Nephi 26:20-21, accents added)
"**20** And the Gentiles are lifted up in the pride of their eyes, and

have **stumbled**, because of the greatness of **their stumbling block**, that **they have built up many churches**; nevertheless, they put down the power and miracles of God, and **preach up unto themselves their own wisdom and their own learning**, that they may get gain and grind upon the face of the poor.
21 And there are **many churches** built up which **cause** envyings, and **strifes**, and malice."

Learning Points:
   A. The results of the purposeful lack of information in the Holy Bible and the adjusting of the ordinances is that the Gentiles have had a Reformation Period, then multiple Great Awakening Periods. They have splintered into thousands of churches. That...is a **great stumbling block**. (See: https://en.wikipedia.org/wiki/Great_Awakening)
   B. Some of these splintered churches **cause envyings**. Have you ever heard of a church preaching ways to wealth and to envy wealth? I have. I won't elaborate.
   C. Some of these splintered churches **cause strifes**. Really... strifes? Have you ever heard of a church preaching hate? I have. I'll leave it at that.
   D. Some of these splintered churches cause malice. The dictionary.com definition of *malice* is "desire to inflict injury, harm, or suffering on another". This sounds like the same churches preaching strifes.

How many churches exactly? The various denominations from some sources number above 33,000 worldwide. I think those numbers are dubious. However, one could safely say more than 200-700 denominations exist in America directly. And that number may prove to be low, as shown below.

Religious Affiliation of The U.S.A. In The Late 1700s and Early 1800s

This page on Wikipedia has a lot of solid information about the growth of denominations in the U.S.A.

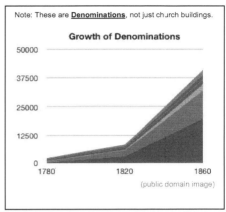

(See: https://en.wikipedia.org/wiki/Christianity_in_the_United_States)

God The Father is not a God of confusion. There is order to his organization. And a few early Christian thinkers saw a problem developing as well. (See Appendix 2: Recognizing The Great Apostasy)

Nephi Writes To The Believing Gentiles

Nephi writes to us, **the Believing Gentiles**, and those who will read the Book of Mormon; which plates were started with Nephi's own hand. In Chapter 28, Nephi gives us **the exact language that this stumbling block will produce** out of the **Unbelieving Gentiles'** own mouths...

(2 Nephi 28:3, accents added)

"**3** For it shall come to pass **in that day** that the churches which are built up, and **not unto the Lord**, when the one shall say unto the other: Behold, I, **I am the Lord's**; and the others shall say: I, **I am the Lord's**; and thus shall **every one** say that hath built up churches, and **not unto the Lord**—"

It is what it is. I personally grew up among many people that went to many different churches. They are my friends. I was hoping for a happy ending here. However, I have read enough of the scriptures to know the next part of the story. And it isn't good.

(2 Nephi 28:16-20, accents added)

"**16** Wo unto them that turn aside **the just for a thing of naught** and **revile against that which is good**, and say that **it is of no worth**! For the day shall come that the Lord God will speedily visit the inhabitants of the earth, and **in that day that they are fully ripe in iniquity, they shall perish**.

17 But behold, if the inhabitants of the earth **shall repent** of their wickedness and abominations **they shall not be destroyed**, saith the Lord of Hosts.

18 But behold, **that great and abominable church, the whore of all the earth, must tumble to the earth, and great must be the fall thereof.**

19 For **the kingdom of the devil** must shake, and **they which belong to it** must needs be **stirred up unto repentance**, or the devil will grasp them with his everlasting chains, and they are stirred up to anger and perish;

20 For behold, **at that day** shall he rage in the hearts of the children of men, and stir them up to anger **against that which is good.**"

What is the "thing that is just" that is being cast out from among the various belief systems of the Gentiles as a "thing of naught." What "good" thing are they being angry against?

There appear a few things in these verses that are important to our topic.

1. The Bible-Believing Gentiles are related to the Whore Church - Babylon The Great, unfortunately. I will not venture further.
2. **There is repentance.** This point is good. **Real good.** The Gentiles on The American Continent simply need to repent of false traditions and join the one true Church of Jesus Christ through baptism to receive a remission of their sins. Done. (The Gentiles that repent are classed as "Believing Gentiles." There are 2 sections "Believing Gentiles" and "Unbelieving Gentiles" as shown above.)
3. The "good thing" that is "just" is The Book of Mormon itself. And by extension the Church of Jesus Christ carrying it forth to the world. The reason we know this…is in the next few verses, and shown in Chapter 29.

The "good thing" that the Unbelieving Gentiles will eventually fight against in the future Great Persecution Period is shown below.

(2 Nephi 28:27-29, accents added)

> "**27** Yea, wo be unto him that saith: We have **received, and we need no more**!
>
> **28** And in fine, wo unto all those who tremble, and are angry because of **the truth of God**! For behold, he that is built upon the rock receiveth it with gladness; and he that is built upon a sandy foundation trembleth lest he shall fall.
>
> **29** Wo be unto him that shall say: <u>**We have received the word of God, and we need no more of the word of God, for we have enough!**</u>"

The "extra" Word of God that has come forth outside The Holy Bible is precisely the problem for the unbelieving Gentile.

Here is the classic scripture that is hard to miss for the person reading The Book of Mormon for the first time, as I did...

> (2 Nephi 29:3-4, accents added)
>
> "**3** And because my words shall hiss forth—many of **the Gentiles** shall say: <u>**A Bible! A Bible! We have got a Bible, and there cannot be any more Bible**</u>.
>
> **4** But thus saith the Lord God: **O fools, they shall have a Bible**; and it shall proceed forth from the Jews, mine ancient covenant people. And what thank they the Jews **for the Bible which they receive from them**? Yea, what do the **Gentiles** mean? Do they remember the travails, and the labors, and the pains of the Jews, and **their diligence unto me, in bringing forth salvation unto the Gentiles**?"

Apparently, most people have forgotten that the original Church of Jesus Christ in 33 A.D. was formed with 12 Apostles, **all Jewish by birth**. And that we now live in the Times of the Gentiles. But, there was a **beginning** to that time…and it was with the 12 **Jewish born** Apostles of The Lamb.

Remember, the Lord said that The Bible proceeds from the Jews to the Gentiles. The Old Testament was created of all Israel, but The Jews did preserve the writings through the Kingdom of Judah. We don't have the scriptures through the Lost 10 Tribes nor the Kingdom of Israel of the North. That is not where our scriptures come from. Our Old Testament does come through the Kingdom of Judah in the South. **They preserved it for the Gentiles**.

The New Testament also came from the Jews themselves at 33AD, when many of them converted to Christianity after seeing what Christ and the Apostles had done. So, the New Testament comes through the bloodline of Judah as well. And those new Christians of Jewish descent suffered mighty persecution at the hands of the Roman Empire and Jewish High Priests of the day. Remember Saul/Paul was a Jewish religious police enforcer. (Have a look at the martyr language around Seal #5 in the Book of Revelation, as seen above.)

Also, the European Gentiles did receive the books of The Holy Bible from the Christians of original Jewish descent - Peter, James, and John. And don't forget Paul of the Tribe of Benjamin – The missionary to the Gentiles.

How Is The Stumbling Block Removed From The Gentiles?

How does an unbelieving Gentile become a believing Gentile? As many of the Unbelieving Gentiles who repent are numbered among Israel.

> (2 Nephi 30:2-3, accents added)
> "**2** For behold, I say unto you that **as many of the Gentiles as will repent are the covenant people of the Lord**; and as many of the Jews as will not repent shall be cast off; for the Lord covenanteth with none save it be with them **that repent and believe in his Son**, who is the Holy One of Israel.
> **3** And now, I would prophesy somewhat more concerning the Jews and the Gentiles. For after **the book (Book of Mormon)** of which I have spoken shall come forth, and be **written unto the Gentiles**, and **sealed up again** unto the Lord, there shall be **many which shall believe the words which are written**; and **they** shall carry them forth unto the remnant of our seed."

Learning Points:
A. The Believing Gentiles will carry the book to the world…and to Israel, including Lehi's children. The Believing Gentiles are the custodians of The Book of Mormon because they believe the continuing words of God written in the book.

Then reverting back to 1st Nephi chapter 14, we see the resolution of SOME of the Gentiles getting the stumbling block removed.

(1 Nephi 14:1-2 accents added)

"**1** And it shall come to pass, that **if the Gentiles shall hearken unto the Lamb of God in that day** that he shall manifest himself unto them in word, and also in power, in very deed, unto the <u>**taking away of their stumbling blocks**</u>—
2 And harden not their hearts against the Lamb of God, <u>**they shall be numbered among the seed of thy father**</u>; yea, <u>**they shall be numbered among the house of Israel**</u>; and they shall be **a blessed people** <u>**upon the promised land forever**</u>; they shall be **no more** brought down **into captivity**; and the house of Israel shall no more be confounded."

This scripture seems to apply to some of the **Unbelieving Gentiles becoming new Believing Gentiles**. The <u>**new Believing Gentiles shall be counted among the House of Israel.**</u> This is a super important point. Think about this.

And why are the Believing Gentiles considered numbered among Lehi's seed? It may be because the Believing Gentiles are plugging into the scriptural roots of Lehi's seed…The Book of Mormon. (More on this roots topic to come.)

So, if that is the case, then what of the **Unbelieving Gentiles**? What happens to them upon the promised land, if the Believing Gentiles are to be a blessed people there forever?

What Is The Future of The UnBelieving Gentiles Upon The Promised Land?

The belief systems of our day 2019 that reject further revelation from God will eventually join forces and captivate those Believing Gentiles during The Great Persecution Period, yet future. (See "United Nations of Churches" in *The Last Days Timeline – Volume 1* - Appendix 1)

Then, at their persecution peak, the judgments of God come upon them. In America **first**; then later in Europe and around the world. (See: *The Last Days Timeline – Volume 1*)

> DISCLAIMER: None of these remarks are about any particular denomination of Christianity. The above materials are coming from scripture. I have feelings of gratitude for the Christian world in giving me my first understandings of Christ. Also, I have many friends, family, and associates that are Christians of different faiths. I wish no ill will upon anyone or any denomination, only the blessings of God.

In the past, the Jewish nation had **stumbled** because of their animal sacrifices and their table. They rejected the tree of Jesus Christ's true church which was among them. Their natural branch was removed from the tree.

In the future, when the Times of the Gentiles are complete, the Gentiles will **stumble** by rejecting the fullness of Jesus Christ's true church which is among them. Their wild branches will be removed from the tree.

The pattern will be complete.

12. Was The Gentile Great Apostasy Prophesied?

Jesus The Christ came to the combined children of Lehi that survived the destruction at 33 A.D.

During that time Jesus shared the doctrines of the new Christian Church on the American Continent. It was founded and started with the Nephite 12 disciples.

Jesus spent multiple days with the Nephites in the Land of Bountiful.

One specific doctrine that was taught was the **Law of Consecration**.

Multiple generations of The People of God would fully live the Gospel. Yet it would eventually come to an end.

That end would be through the 3rd generation and many of the 4th generation. But soon after that, destruction would come upon their children. This would be describing Mormon and Moroni's day of 300-400 A.D.

> (3rd Nephi 27:30-32 accents added)
> "**30** And now, behold, my joy is great, even unto fulness, because of you, and also this generation; yea, and even the Father rejoiceth, and also all the holy angels, because of you and this generation; for none of them are lost.
> **31** Behold, I would that ye should understand; for I mean them who are now alive of **this generation**; and none of them are lost; and in them I have fulness of joy.

32 But behold, it sorroweth me because of **the fourth generation from this generation**, for they are led away captive by him even as was the son of perdition; for **they will sell me for silver and for gold**, and for that which moth doth corrupt and which thieves can break through and steal. And in **that day will I visit them, even in turning their works upon their own heads**."

And this same doctrine of 3-4 generations until the destruction was also preached by Samuel the Lamanite in 6 B.C.

(Helaman 13:4-10 accents added)
"**4** And it came to pass that they would not suffer that he should enter into the city; therefore he went and got upon the wall thereof, and stretched forth his hand and cried with a loud voice, and **prophesied** unto the people whatsoever things the Lord put into his heart.
5 And he said unto them: Behold, I, Samuel, a Lamanite, do speak the words of the Lord which he doth put into my heart; and behold he hath put it into my heart to say unto this people that the sword of justice hangeth over this people; and **four hundred years pass not away save the sword of justice falleth upon this people.**
6 Yea, heavy destruction awaiteth this people, and it surely cometh unto this people, and nothing can save this people save it be repentance and faith on the Lord Jesus Christ, who surely shall come into the world, and shall suffer many things and shall be slain for his people.

7 And behold, **an angel of the Lord hath declared it unto me**, and he did bring glad tidings to my soul. And behold, I was sent unto you to declare it unto you also, that ye might have glad tidings; but behold ye would not receive me.
8 Therefore, **thus saith the Lord**: Because of the hardness of the hearts of the people of the Nephites, except they repent I will take away my word from them, and I will withdraw my Spirit from them, and I will suffer them **no longer**, and **I will turn the hearts of their brethren against them.**
9 And **four hundred years** shall not pass away before I will cause that they shall be smitten; yea, **I will visit them with the sword and with famine and with pestilence.**
10 Yea, I will visit them in my fierce anger, and there shall be those of **the fourth generation** who shall live, **of your enemies**, to **behold your utter destruction**; and this shall surely come except ye repent, saith the Lord; and those of the **fourth generation shall visit your destruction.**"

And this same doctrine of 3-4 generations until the destruction was known by Nephi too…

(2nd Nephi 26:8-10 accents added)
"**8** But behold, the righteous that hearken unto the words of the prophets, and destroy them not, but look forward unto Christ with steadfastness **for the signs** which are given, notwithstanding all persecution—behold, they are they which shall not perish.
9 But the Son of Righteousness **shall appear unto them**; and he shall heal them, and they shall have peace with him, **until three generations shall have passed away**, and **many**

of the fourth generation shall have passed away in righteousness.

10 And **when** these things have passed away a **speedy destruction cometh unto my people**; for, notwithstanding the pains of my soul, **I have seen it**; wherefore, I know that it shall come to pass; and they sell themselves for naught; for, for the reward of their pride and their foolishness they shall reap **destruction**; for because they yield unto the devil and choose works of darkness rather than light, therefore they must go down to hell."

The Law of Moses was completed. And the new Christian religion was now beginning among this Tribe of Israel on the Americas. Yet, it was only to last 3-4 generations.

The Nephites Knew When Their Time Was UP. But What About The Apostles of the Original Church of Jesus Christ?

In 1964, Hugh Nibley gave a talk about the books of the Apocrypha titled The Forty Day Ministry of Jesus After The Resurrection

He documented many points of doctrine that were in the King James Version of the Apocrypha and some other books that were part of the ancient Church of Jesus Christ but have faded since that day…until the restoration by Joseph Smith Jr.

One of the most fascinating doctrines taught was that the Church of Jesus Christ in the meridian of time would not last more than a few generations. Have a look at my notes from the audio recording below.

(From my paraphrased notes on *Forty Day Ministry* talk Part 1 by Hugh Nibley 1964 (starting 33m,20s))

(paraphrased) "Now the most conspicuous single teaching of the 40 days is…the thing they talk most about **is the future of the church**…the Apostles ask the Master, "**What lays ahead** of them about the work that they are engaged."

In reply, the Lord paints a simply **appalling picture**. He tells them about **the Great Apostasy** in detail. There is indeed a future source of comfort and joy, but it is **all** on the other side. **Not in this world**.

The Apostles protest…this is a glorious time of the resurrection, why are you talking about gloom and death?

The Apostles themselves ask why are we doing all this work for only a few converts? Will all of this work be taken away?

Jesus answers and says it is not for the Apostles to say. That is the will of the Father. He will decide.

And who is lost is lost and who is saved is saved.

The Lord is **uncompromising in his predictions of gloom**.

These predictions of gloom are specific to the Apostles. The **danger is not from the pagan Roman society**, but from the **newly forming Christians themselves**. The destruction will come **from inside the Church**.

Jesus says specifically that the church will be **divided into 2 parties**. With **complete victory on the part of the corrupters over the party of the Saints**. He says specifically it will be **completed within 2 generations**. Jesus says that in multiple locations in the text. And it all happens on the inside of the church. The sheep turn to wolves and lead the church astray. This is called, "**The wintertime of the just.**" Which lays ahead.

Lucifer…the one that leads the world astray takes over for a long period of darkness. Ruling falsely under the name of Christ.

This is the common picture that Jesus gives of the future. And nobody liked the picture. Not even the Apostles.

Nobody wanted to believe it. Just like the "resurrection of the flesh problem."

In the 2nd generation of the church fathers, they see these negative apostasy events coming to pass in actual fulfillment. And **they accepted it.**"

There is much more. Download both parts to this whole Hugh Nibley talk at: www.LastDaysTimeline.com/hugh-nibley-apocrypha/

The generations of good fruit the new Gentiles would produce, was prophesied to be short. **Just 2 generations.**

All came to pass as this Prophecy of The Tame and Wild Olive Trees stated from the pen of Zenos thousands of years ago.

Now let's catch up with the ongoing apostasy of the Lost 10 Tribes of Israel.

What is their church status like in this 1820 visit of the Master and the Servant to their remote part of the Vineyard?

13. What is Happening to The Lost 10 Tribes of Israel in 1820 AD?

Not only did the Gentiles spoil the main tree with Bad Fruit of different types with a maturing Great Apostasy, but the Lost 10 Tribes and the children of Lehi are undergoing a terrible apostasy at the same time.

> (Jacob 5:38-39 accents added)
> "**38** And it came to pass that the Lord of the vineyard said unto his servant: Let us go down into **the nethermost parts of the vineyard**, and behold **if** the natural branches have also brought forth **evil fruit**.
> **39** And it came to pass that they went down into the nethermost parts of the vineyard. And it came to pass that they beheld that **the fruit of the natural branches had become corrupt also**; yea, **the first** and **the second** and also **the last**; and they had **all become corrupt**."

Learning Points:
   A. At this time 1820 A.D., it appears that the Lost 10 Tribes living in the North also suffered a Great Apostasy as well.
   B. The Tribe of Reuben and Simeon had become corrupted in doctrine in 1820 A.D.
   C. This word "corrupt fruit" is not the same as the word "bad fruit" or "evil fruit". It seems to be a different situation than what happened to the Gentiles in Europe and America. BUT, the effect was the same. The Lost 10 Tribes and the children of

Lehi in the Americas were all Bad Fruit. Not worthy of preserving in glory.
D. All the natural tribes of Israel were "corrupt" in doctrine in 1820 A.D.

Something Special Happened to The Children of Lehi?

After looking at the other Tribes of Israel (the Natural Branches); the Master/Lord shares identifying information about the children of Lehi. Which helps us identify them.

Remember, Jacob is reading Zenos' writings to a large group of Nephites around 550BC. This is far before Jacob's own children were wiped out. Jacob wanted them to know the end from the beginning.

Our Father in Heaven has done the same for us in 2019; this is one of the reasons why He had His prophets declare unto us these prophecies for our day; that we might **be prepared for the future** and **have faith** in the word of God.

> (Jacob 5:40-45 accents added)
> "**40** And the **wild fruit** of <u>**the last**</u> had **overcome** that <u>**part**</u> of the tree which brought forth **good fruit**, even that <u>**the branch had withered away and died.**</u>
> **41** And it came to pass that the Lord of the vineyard **wept**, and said unto the servant: What could I have done more for my vineyard?
> **42** Behold, I knew that all the fruit of the vineyard, **save it were these**, had become corrupted. And now **these** which have

once brought forth good fruit have also become corrupted; and now **all the trees of my vineyard are good for nothing save it be to be hewn down and cast into the fire**.

43 And behold **this last**, whose **branch hath withered away**, I did plant in a **good spot of ground**; yea, even that which was choice unto me above all other parts of the land of my vineyard.

44 And thou beheldest that I also **cut down that which cumbered this spot of ground**, that I might plant this tree in the stead thereof.

45 And thou beheldest that **a part** thereof brought forth **good fruit**, and a part thereof brought forth **wild fruit**; and **because I plucked not the branches thereof and cast them into the fire, behold, they have overcome the good branch that it hath withered away**."

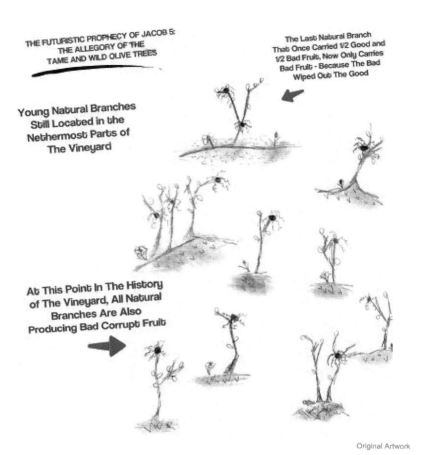

Original Artwork

Learning Points:

A. The "Lamanites" had overcome the "Nephites in the final struggle around 400 A.D. This struggle was after the last check by The Father and The Son in the Vineyard in 60-200 A.D. Yet, before this 1820 A.D. Vineyard check. This fits real history.

B. The Master in the prophecy **hoped** that "these" Natural Branches of Israel would save the day and produce good fruit. All the other trees in the whole vineyard were already corrupted. This would represent all the other peoples on planet Earth. (Note: in reality, The Father doesn't "hope." He **knows** the end from the beginning. Else how was this prophecy ever uttered? The future is known by our Father in Heaven.)

C. The Father is **ready to burn the entire Earth** and scrap this whole round of creation. It was **that** bad in 1820 A.D.

D. The Father is lamenting that the Nephite branch was destroyed by the Lamanite branch in 400 A.D. Mormon and Moroni recorded this destruction in The Book of Mormon.

E. **The Jaredites** – The children of Lehi's natural tree branch was planted in the Americas. In 590 B.C. the boat landing location was **southern Jaredite territory**. The Master/Lord **cut down the Jaredites** to plant the seed of Joseph in the Americas.

F. **The Plan** – Remember the plan to keep the Lamanites alive a little longer was The Servant's plan, not the Master's plan. The Father wanted to pluck the bad branch up and burn it. The Lamanite/Nephite dissenters, were **the only bad branch** of Israel or Gentiles in the previous 33 A.D. Vineyard check. But, the Father doesn't blame the Son. It was the Father's final decision to keep the Lamanites around. Ultimately, at this 1820 A.D. Vineyard check, the Lamanite/Nephite dissenters had already killed off the Nephites and their branch withered away long ago.

The ultimate problem is that at this moment of 1820 A.D. there is no Good Fruit left in the Vineyard.

The whole Vineyard is corrupt and wasted. The Master/Father is very upset…and saddened.

He is looking to find out who did this.

14. An Enemy Hath Done This

After the 1820 A.D. visit, when the Gentile fruit has been demonstrated to be bad, The Master/Father asks how this could have happened.

> (Jacob 5:46-47 accents added)
> "**46** And now, behold, notwithstanding all the care which we have taken of my vineyard, **the trees** thereof have become corrupted, that they bring forth **no good fruit**; and <u>these</u> I had hoped to preserve, to have laid up fruit thereof against the season, unto mine own self. But, behold, **they have become like unto the wild olive tree**, and they are of no worth but to be <u>**hewn down and cast into the fire**</u>; and it grieveth me that I should lose them.
> **47** But what could I have done more in my vineyard? Have I slackened mine hand, that I have not nourished it? Nay, I have nourished it, and I have digged about it, and I have pruned it, and I have dunged it; and I have stretched forth mine hand almost all the day long, and the **end draweth nigh**. And it grieveth me that I should hew down **all the trees** of my vineyard, and **cast them into the fire** that they should be burned. <u>**Who is it that has corrupted my vineyard?**</u>"

Learning Points:

A. At this point of 1820 A.D. in the timeline, 100% of the nations of people in the Vineyard have become corrupted; without Jesus Christ's true ordinances and church doctrines in the world. Jews, Lost Tribes of Israel, Gentiles, Heathen, Idol worshipers; all of them were corrupted in doctrine. All of humanity. This is the sad fact of the allegory.

B. The 12 Tribes of Israel had all become corrupted in doctrine, just like the Gentiles.

C. The Father/Master/Lord wants to hew down **all** the nations and **cast them into the fire** early, before the season is over. To start over. This is the **justice and judgment** of The Father. And He is **just**. However, Jesus/The Servant/Mediator has another idea; one of **grace and saving**. This time it works; as we shall see.

    a. **Author's Analysis:** In the Plan of Salvation, always remember The Father **represents justice** and the Savior **represents mercy**. This justice /VS/ mercy concept lines up in this prophecy too.

D. **Who is it that has corrupted my Vineyard?** – This question begs the answer of Lucifer/Satan/The Devil. However, I think the real answer is given in the allegory itself in the next verse.

How Did The Prideful Leaders Take Doctrine Creation Unto Themselves?

In 1820 A.D., there was a problem. Joseph Smith stated that there were just too many churches in the New York Burned-Over District to make a clear choice. It was the time of the 2nd Great Awakening in America and even further to Europe. (See: https://en.wikipedia.org/wiki/Great_Awakening)

The doctrine they were preaching seems to all be from the Bible. But,...not quite from the Bible.

That was the problem.

Let's see what Jesus says is the problem in 1820 A.D. as He and The Father **both** appear to Joseph Smith in The First Vision.

> (Joseph Smith-History 1:17-23 accents added)
> "**17** It no sooner appeared than I found myself delivered from the enemy which held me bound. When the light rested upon me I saw **two Personages**, whose brightness and glory defy all description, standing above me in the air. One of them spake unto me, calling me by name and said, pointing to the other—
> **This is My Beloved Son. Hear Him!**
> **18** My object in going to inquire of the Lord was to know **which of all the sects was right**, that I might know which to join. No sooner, therefore, did I get possession of myself, so as to be able to speak, than I asked the Personages who stood above me in the light, which of all the sects was right (for at this time it had never entered into my heart that all were wrong)—and which I should join.
> **19** I was answered that I must join **none of them**, for they were **all wrong**; and the Personage who addressed me said that **all their creeds were an abomination in his sight**; that **those professors** were **all corrupt**; that: "they draw near to me with their lips, but their hearts are far from me, they **teach**

for doctrines the commandments of men**, having **a form of godliness**, but they **deny the power thereof.**"

20 He again forbade me to join with any of them; and many other things did he say unto me, which I cannot write at this time. When I came to myself again, I found myself lying on my back, looking up into heaven. When the light had departed, I had no strength; but soon recovering in some degree, I went home. And as I leaned up to the fireplace, mother inquired what the matter was. I replied, "Never mind, all is well—I am well enough off." I then said to my mother, "I have learned for myself that **Presbyterianism is not true**." It seems as though the adversary was aware, at a very early period of my life, that I was destined to prove a disturber and an annoyer of his kingdom; else why should the powers of darkness combine against me? Why the opposition and persecution that arose against me, almost in my infancy?

21 Some few days after I had this vision, I happened to be in company with one of the **Methodist preachers**, who was very active in the before mentioned religious excitement; and, conversing with him on the subject of religion, I took occasion to give him an account of the vision which I had had. I was greatly surprised at his behavior; he treated my communication not only lightly, but with great contempt, saying it was **all of the devil**, that there were **no such things as visions or revelations in these days**; that all such things had **ceased with the Apostles**, and that there would **never be any more of them.**

22 I soon found, however, that my telling the story had excited a great deal of prejudice against me **among professors of**

religion, and was the cause of great persecution, which continued to increase; and though I was an obscure boy, only between fourteen and fifteen years of age, and my circumstances in life such as to make a boy of no consequence in the world, **yet men of high standing would take notice sufficient to excite the public mind against me,** and **create a bitter persecution**; and this was common among **all the sects—all united** to persecute me.

23 It caused me serious reflection then, and often has since, how very strange it was that an obscure boy, of a little over fourteen years of age, and one, too, who was doomed to the necessity of obtaining a scanty maintenance by his daily labor, should be thought a character of sufficient importance **to attract the attention of <u>the great ones</u> of the most popular sects of the day**, and in a manner to create in them a spirit of the **most bitter persecution and reviling**. But strange or not, so it was, and it was often the cause of great sorrow to myself."

Learning Points:

A. The Father and The Son **both** speak in 1820. They have **both** come down to the Vineyard and had a work to do.

B. Jesus commanded Joseph to **<u>join "none of them".</u>** Their creeds were abominations. The "professors" or leaders of the religions were "all **corrupt**". Much like all the fruit of the Vineyard had become **100% corrupted**. Including the Gentile branches grafted onto the main olive tree of the Church of Jesus Christ.

C. The quote of Jesus is a combination of Isaiah 29:13 and 2 Timothy 3:5. We will look at these next.
D. The Methodist preacher and others, claim the vision is "all of the devil". This often happened to Paul the apostle when he was preaching the truths of God. And also to the Nephite prophets when they were preaching to the people. Even Jesus himself was accused of possessing a Luciferian spirit. People often claim the truth is of the devil. Don't let this disparage you when this happens in your life.
E. The great leaders of religion of the day in New York State and beyond kept persecuting the truth of Joseph Smith Jr., being called as a prophet of God, until they murdered him.

Discover the people who led that raid into the small jailhouse in Carthage Illinois Jun 27 1844, in the book: *The Fate of the Persecutors of the Prophet Joseph Smith* by Lundwall.

(Note 1: there are some things in Lundwall's book which are outlandish. However, about the **recorded quoted accounts** of those that did the deed to Joseph Smith Jr., Lundwall appears to be spot-on. Note 2: Dallin H. Oaks, **before** he was an apostle, wrote an "Afterword" in his book *Carthage Conspiracy* (1975) that tried to handle the **recorded quoted accounts** of Lundwall's book to show they were a myth. However, they were recorded quoted accounts. So, ultimately some of the people who attacked Joseph Smith Jr. had a rotten death, while others had a successful career life. Nothing is 100%, as shown by both of these books.)

The quote by Jesus to the boy Joseph Smith Jr. about **why** he is not to join any of the churches fulfills a 2000-year-old prophecy by the apostle Timothy in the New Testament.

(2 Timothy 3:1-9 accents added)
"1 This know also, that in **the last days** perilous times shall come.
2 For men shall be lovers of their own selves, covetous, boasters, proud, blasphemers, disobedient to parents, unthankful, **unholy**,
3 Without natural affection, trucebreakers, **false accusers**, incontinent, fierce, **despisers of those that are good**,
4 Traitors, heady, **highminded**, lovers of pleasures more than lovers of God;
5 **Having a form of godliness, but denying the power thereof**: from such **turn away**.
6 For of this sort are they which creep into houses, and lead captive silly women laden with sins, led away with divers lusts,
7 **Ever learning, and never able to come to the knowledge of the truth**.
8 Now as Jannes and Jambres withstood Moses, so do **these also resist the truth**: men of **corrupt minds**, **reprobate concerning the faith.**
9 But **they shall proceed no further**: for **their folly** shall be manifest unto all men, as theirs also was."

Learning Points:
- A. Do you think Timothy had prophetic revelation as an apostle of the Lord? (Many people are not familiar with this scripture.)
- B. This is a prophecy of the **last days**.
- C. Since Timothy is speaking of those that **have a form of godliness, but deny the power thereof**, the previous few verses also apply to this group of people that Timothy is speaking of; the "false accusers", the "high minded", and the "despisers of those [people] that are good."
- D. This group shall also be ever learning and **never able** to come to the knowledge of the truth. Also, they shall resist the truth.
    - a. Remember, the Whore Church took away the precious parts of the Bible and the covenants of the Lamb, **before** the Gentiles of the last days ever got to have the Bible.
- E. Men of **corrupt** minds – there is that word again, "corrupt". Just as 100% of the fruit is corrupt in The Master's vineyard. They are also "reprobate concerning the faith."
    - a. These short phrases are framing words. There are words concerning religion and the leaders of religions throughout this whole set of verses. Delivered thousands of years ago from Timothy in 40-50 A.D. (See Appendix 2: Recognizing The Great Apostasy)

The quote by Jesus above also fulfills the ancient prophecy of Isaiah in the Old Testament.

(Isaiah 29:12-14 accents added)

"**12** And the book is delivered to him that is not learned, saying, Read this, I pray thee: and he saith, **I am not learned**.

13 ¶ Wherefore the Lord said, Forasmuch as <u>**this people draw near me with their mouth, and with their lips do honour me, but have removed their heart far from me, and their fear toward me is taught by the precept of men**</u>:

14 Therefore, behold, I will proceed to do a marvelous work among this people, even **a marvellous work and a wonder**: for the **wisdom of** <u>**their wise men**</u> **shall perish**, and the **understanding of** <u>**their prudent men**</u> **shall be hid**."

These verses are also **the very last Isaiah chapter** that Nephi, son of Lehi, brother of Jacob, inserted into 2nd Nephi in the Book of Mormon. Notice some **big** differences.

(2 Nephi 27:19-26 accents added)

"**19** Wherefore it shall come to pass, that the Lord God will deliver again the book and the words thereof to him that is not learned; and the man that is not learned shall say: **I am not learned.**

20 Then shall the Lord God say unto him: The learned shall not read them, for **they have rejected them**, and I am able to do mine own work; wherefore thou shalt read the words which I shall give unto thee.

21 Touch not the things which are sealed, for I will bring them forth in mine own due time; for I will show unto the children of men that I am able to do mine own work.

22 Wherefore, when thou hast read the words which I have commanded thee, and obtained the witnesses which I have promised unto thee, then shalt thou seal up the book again, and hide it up unto me, that I may preserve **the words which thou hast not read**, until I shall see fit in mine own wisdom to reveal **all things** unto the children of men.

23 For behold, I am God; and I am a God of miracles; and I will show unto the world that I am the same yesterday, today, and forever; and I work not among the children of men save it be according to their faith.

24 And again it shall come to pass that the Lord shall say unto him that shall read the words that shall be delivered him:

25 <u>Forasmuch as this people draw near unto me with their mouth, and with their lips do honor me, but have removed their hearts far from me, and their fear towards me is taught by the precepts of men</u>—

26 Therefore, I will proceed to do a marvelous work among this people, yea, **a marvelous work and a wonder**, for the wisdom of **<u>their wise and learned shall perish</u>**, and the understanding of **<u>their prudent</u>** shall be hid."

Did you notice the verses in the middle that directly point to **a latter-day unlearned man that will bring God's work to pass**? Those identification verses are completely missing from our Bibles today.

The Whore Church removed them. They speak of **<u>an unlearned man</u>** doing God's work in the future. Not a member of the professional clergy.

(For information on The Whore Church see: *The Last Days Timeline*)

The Rejection of Zenos' Prophecy By The New Gentile Church

So, why was this prophecy of Zenos taken out by the Jews and the early Christians.

It seems that the reason Zenos was struck out was because of the direct revelations of Christ being crucified by his own people (extremely unpopular), and this giant prophecy of the future of Israel.

First cut out by the Jews, because it makes them look bad.

Then cut out by the early Gentile Church, because it makes them look bad. (unpopular on all sides)

Next, we see what the Father's plan **that extends <u>well beyond</u> 2019**.

SECTION 4: The Plan For Restoration Is Presented

Original Artwork

15. The High Branches Have Overcome The Roots. How Does That Happen?

The Servant answers the Master's question about who corrupted the vineyard. It isn't a pretty answer.

The culprit was the Gentile Whore Church and her harlots.

Remember Lucifer started this church and it will eventually cause The Great Persecution Period upon The Church of Jesus Christ. This marks the end of The Times of The Gentiles. Their branches will then **start** to be burned.

> (Jacob 5:48-51 accents added)
> "**48** And it came to pass that **the servant said unto his master**: Is it not **the loftiness** of thy vineyard—have not **the branches thereof overcome the roots which are good**? And **because** the branches have **overcome the roots** thereof, behold **they grew faster than the strength of the roots, taking strength unto themselves**. Behold, I say, is not this **the cause** that the trees of thy vineyard have become corrupted?
> **49** And it came to pass that the Lord of the vineyard said unto the servant: Let us go to and **hew down the trees of the vineyard and cast them into the fire**, that they shall not cumber the ground of my vineyard, for I have done all. What could I have done more for my vineyard?

50 But, behold, **the servant said unto the Lord** of the vineyard: **Spare it a little longer.**

51 And the Lord said: Yea, **I will spare it a little longer**, for it grieveth me that I should lose the trees of my vineyard."

Learning Points:

A. The Servant defined **the real cause** of the bad fruit in all the Vineyard. It wasn't "a person" that came and hurt the vineyard trees. It was a **problematic situation of "growth" of the branches themselves**.

B. It appears that we are looking at the main natural tree, but the Servant and Lord/Master are talking about "the Vineyard" as a whole. Keep that in mind.

C. The problem of the main natural tree was that the new Gentile branches that were grafted on, after they produced "good fruit", **eventually morphed** and overcame the natural **roots** and **"taking strength unto themselves."** This would be the very definition of The Great Apostasy. That the Gentile Whore Church **changed the ordinances and scripture roots themselves**. Just as Nephi saw in his grand future vision. And Nephi wasn't the only human to have seen this problem. (See Appendix 2: *Recognizing The Great Apostasy* for many quotes of early thinkers)

D. The Master/Lord/Father's **justice is ready to take hold**. He is ready to scrap the whole vineyard and start over. Cutting down every tree and casting them **all** into the fire. This was in 1820 A.D. Just before the restoration of the gospel of Jesus Christ to the Earth.

E. It was the Servant/Jesus that steps in **as mediator** once again to save the trees and branches of the Vineyard. This is showing the Servant in **the role of mediator** and **savior** of the trees and branches. This plan works this time and brings forth good fruit once again. (Thank goodness)

F. This broad blanket statement by The Servant/Jesus about **the cause** of why the whole vineyard produced bad fruit, also implies that The Lost 10 Tribes of Israel in the North underwent an apostasy away from true Christian religion at the same time that the Gentiles nations underwent the Great Apostasy.

16. The Idea is Set. Let`s Discover What The Plan is For Our Future Beyond 2019

Once the idea was set to save the Vineyard "just a little longer," there was a chance that things would work out well.

The Father continues and makes a plan with Jesus to possibly bring good fruit into the Vineyard once again.

Let's discover what the elements of the plan are…

> (Jacob 5:52-54 accents added)
> "**52** Wherefore, let us take of **the branches of <u>these</u> which I have planted in the nethermost parts of my vineyard**, and let us **graft them into the tree from whence they came**; and let us **<u>pluck</u>** from the tree **those branches whose fruit is most bitter**, and **graft in the natural branches** of the tree **<u>in the stead</u>** thereof.
> **53** And this will I do that the tree may not perish, that, perhaps, I may **preserve unto myself the roots** thereof for mine own purpose.
> **54** And, behold, **<u>the roots of the natural branches</u>** of the tree which I planted whithersoever I would **are yet alive**; wherefore, that I may **preserve them <u>also</u>** for mine own purpose, I will take of the branches of **<u>this tree</u>**, and I will **graft them in <u>unto them</u>**. Yea, I will graft in **<u>unto them</u>** the branches of **<u>their mother tree</u>**, that I may **preserve the roots <u>also</u>** unto mine own self, that when they shall be sufficiently strong perhaps

they may bring forth **good fruit** unto me, and I may **yet have glory** in the fruit of my vineyard."

Learning Points:
    A. This plan has several components.
    B. #1 - to take the natural branches of Israel (The Lost 10 Tribes, children of Lehi, and Jews) and **re-graft** them back into the main Natural Tree.
    C. #2 - while grafting, take out the wild Gentile branches that are **most bitter**, and in their stead, plant the Tribes of Israel.
        a. This would mean that when the Times of the Gentiles are **completed**, the **Unbelieving Gentile people will be removed** and Tribes of Israel will be planted **in their promised lands.** Including the Believing Gentiles too. This land of the Americas is to be a place to dwell safely forever.
        b. The **worst** of the Gentiles will be plucked first and burned. This is a progression of Gentile destruction. While the restoration of Israel to the Promised Lands is happening over time. This is a **slower process** that happens over time. It is **not fast**. (Remember, this happens **after** the Times of the Gentiles are fulfilled and is describing the takedown of the **4th Beast Kingdom of the Gentiles**. It is yet future to 2019. See *The Last Days Timeline – Volume 1* for details.)
    D. #3 – **The roots of the natural branches** that were in the nethermost parts of the Vineyard ALSO are to be preserved

for the Master. If the roots of the main tree are the scriptures and the word of God, then the roots of these small natural branches in the nethermost parts of the vineyard are most likely also **the scriptures and the word of God unto them**.

E. (v54) The Twister - I have read a few ideas about this verse. The key to understanding it, is to realize **what tree** he was standing next to when he said it. The Master/Father was **standing next to the Mother Tree, while talking about the Natural Trees.** So, the Father is saying that he will take a **Gentile branch** and graft it into one of the **Natural branch tree roots.** Yes. That would be the perfect definition of what has happened with the Ephraimite Gentiles coming out of the world during the Times of the Gentiles and being grafted into The Manasseh Book of Mormon scripture roots and the restoration of the gospel of Jesus Christ by Joseph Smith Jr in 1830 A.D. **Yep, it was there the whole time**.

F. **Good Fruit = Glory** – The word glory is also used here to describe the Master's goal with the good fruit… "glory." So, again we see that the definition of the good fruit is adding glory to The Master/God the Father.

The glory of God is intelligence. And yet, the work and glory of God's mission is to "bring to pass the immortality and eternal life of man."

The most relevant understanding of the glory topic is to realize that with our own future perfected intelligence, we obtain glory, which adds to God's **family glory**.

You have a purpose on this earth. **To become the good fruit of glory.**

The Plan for Our Future to 2019 is Implemented

The grafting plan to save the entire Vineyard is implemented. The Master/Lord/Father and the Servant/Jesus are moving in the Vineyard to make the new plan a reality.

SECTION 5: The Plan For Restoration Is Begun

Original Artwork

17. The Last Days Restoration of Jesus Christ's True Church in The Vineyard Has Begun

When the prophecy of the Tame and Wild Olive Trees was first given by Zenos in the Old Testament of the Bible, almost all of it was still future to him.

However, at this point in the timeline 2019, most of the prophecy is behind us in time.

This section of the prophecy will take us into the Master's actions performed in the modern age, and beyond.

Continuing the factual basis of this study, we will continue to identify the symbolic elements of the allegory. Some are quite surprising…

The Plan For The "Last Work" is Put into Action…A Little

We have seen the plan that was founded just prior to 1820 A.D.

Now, let's see how it will be actually implemented in 1830 A.D.

> (Jacob 5:55-56 accents added)
> "**55** And it came to pass that they took **from the <u>natural tree</u>** which had become wild, and **grafted in unto the natural <u>trees</u>**, which also had become wild.

56 And **they** also took of the natural **trees** which had become wild, and grafted into **their mother tree**."

Learning Points:
  A. Notice the "tree" (singular) /vs/ "trees" (plural). This distinction makes Zenos' words more clear.
  B. This moment is **the first action** after the big planning session. Note that **this is NOT the big main grafting** of Israel to the Mother Tree. This is a small early grafting project. The big one comes in a few verses, which is future to 2019.
  C. (v55) This is the exact moment when the wild branches from the mother tree are grafted in a branch or two into the smaller natural trees around the Vineyard. This is the first action in **the restoration of the Church of Jesus Christ through Joseph Smith Jr. in 1830 A.D.**
     a. Further note that this is **the first action** in the Vineyard after the disastrous 1820 A.D. Vineyard check. In real history, the restoration of Jesus Christ's Church among the American Gentile nation with the Bill of Rights protecting freedom of religion was the first action. Even God the Father and Jesus **both** visited the boy Joseph in the spring of 1820 A.D. Just as the prophecy said…in correct order.
  D. Yet, there are some natural branches being grafted onto the Mother Tree as well. What could that be?
     a. **Author's Analysis**: It appears that this grafting is a return of a natural branch of Israel which had become scattered and corrupted back to the lands of their

inheritance. And that it appears early in the saga of grafting. It is well before the Nation of Zion era. To me, that looks like the Israelites of Jewish descent being returned to the land of their inheritance in the modern nation of Israel starting in 1948. And in 2018, Jerusalem is now their recognized capital; thanks to Donald Trump. Yes. Even that part of world history is contained in this prophecy…and at the right time in the prophecy itself. We are still in the early period of grafting. There is much more to come.

Remember the Tribe of Benjamin. He was the last born youngest son of Jacob/Israel. Because the Tribe of Benjamin was with Judah, Benjamin would have been the last one to leave the holy land in 70 A.D.

Yet, if Benjamin's lineage is intertwined through a few thousand years with Judah, then Benjamin would also have been the 1st Tribe back into the holy land in 1948. Last born, last out, first in.

The first shall be last and the last shall be first.

The Master/Father Gives Further Instructions on "When" The Wild Branches Are to Be Cut Off and Burned

There are further instructions from Father/Master/Lord to Jesus/Servant, after the "doing" has already begun.

In particular, notice the "when" the Gentile branches are to be plucked off?

> (Jacob 5:57-60 accents added)
>
> "**57** And the Lord of the vineyard said unto the servant: **Pluck not** the wild branches from the trees, save it be those which are **most bitter**; **and in them** ye shall graft according to that which I have said.
>
> **58** And we will **nourish again the trees of the vineyard**, and we will **trim up** the branches thereof; and we will **pluck from** the trees those branches which **are ripened, that must perish**, and cast them into **the fire**.
>
> **59** And this I do that, perhaps, **the roots** thereof may take strength because of their goodness; and because of **the change of the branches**, that **the good may overcome the evil**.
>
> **60** And because that I have preserved the natural branches and the roots thereof, and that I have grafted in the natural branches again into their mother tree, and **have preserved the roots of their mother tree**, that, perhaps, the **trees** of my vineyard may bring forth again good fruit; and that I may have **joy** again in the fruit of my vineyard, and, perhaps, that I may **rejoice exceedingly** that I have preserved the **roots** and the **branches** of **the first fruit—**"

Learning Points:
    A. The Father/Master/Lord is also going to **personally** engage in the work of branch replacement. The Father has not fully

delegated the work to Jesus/The Servant. They **both** are engaged in this work.

B. **Answer:** The Servant is to pluck the wild Gentile branches ONLY when they have become most bitter, ripe, a time for them to perish and be cast into the fire. What time is this?

    a. As from the Apostle Paul's writing in Romans Chapter 11, <u>**this time point is when the Fullness of The Gentiles Has Come in.**</u> Or when the Times of the Gentiles is **complete or finished**.

        i. As noted in the book: *The Last Days Timeline* by James T. Prout (this author), this fullness of the *Time of the Gentiles* takes place when the Gentiles persecute and attack The Church of God. Which is yet future, under the 4th Beast Kingdom of the Gentiles with the Whore Church Babylon the Great riding it.

C. The Father/Master/Lord will also do the work of trimming the branches and nourishing the tree. By the past definitions of **hearing God the Father's voice** when he is in the vineyard; during this period of our future to 2019, **Father will once again <u>proclaim his Son</u> and that we should hear Him**.

D. The reason for the switch in branches is so **the root scriptures** may again take great strength and bring again good fruit to the newly transplanted branches of the 12 Tribes of Israel. They shall be slowly transplanted back to the mother tree.

E. The word "trees" (plural) was used to point out that God the Father is not just attempting to save the one mother tree of

Israel, but many more trees in the vineyard as well. Good glorious fruit will eventually come from many trees in the vineyard, as we shall see.

F. Yet, it all starts with the "first fruit" of the 12 Tribes of Israel and the mother tree.

Author's Analysis:

Note the items that we just covered:

1. The Times of the Gentiles is nearly coming to an end in this prophecy. That is the time in which we live in 2019.

2. The Jews have been planted in the land of Israel in 1948. Along with the Tribe of Benjamin which was joined with them. The last son of Jacob was inserted 1st back into the holy land.

3. The 1st Gentile branch was cut from the Mother tree and planted into a natural branch's scriptural roots. This represents the Gentiles, being planted into the scriptural roots of Manasseh as the Children of Lehi; Who wrote the Book of Mormon. This is the Church of Jesus Christ today.

4. There was a short "break" for additional instructions to be given, after these first few graftings and the major work of dunging, pruning, and digging. Including the Servant's new helpers. That additional work hasn't happened yet. (as the next chapter shows).

Special Note: In 2019, we are living during the "break" for special instructions. After the first few grafts, but before the big work

> project begins. Because there hasn't been any additional Gentile branches cut off the tree, nor any more bulk grafting of the tribes of Israel into the Gospel of Jesus Christ. This is the current day 2019.
>
> You now know when you live in the Prophecy of The Tame and Wild Olive Trees.
>
> Use this information to teach your family what comes next in the prophecy and what comes next in the future.

What Does The Ezra's Eagle Prophecy Tell Us About The Gentile Branch's Grafting Order?

This is a big clue.

The Ezra's Eagle Prophecy tells us that there needs to be a future time when The Lion Kingdom from the North will take down the beat-up Eagle Kingdom and clear it out of the Promised Land.

Since we know that there are only 12 Tribes of Israel, there is a finite number of peoples to occupy promised lands.

Most of the tribes have promised lands around modern-day Jerusalem; within several hundred miles in most directions. Judah and the youngest son Benjamin were already grafted in 1948.

Yet, **the Americas were given to the House of Joseph** as promised lands. The House of Joseph contains Ephraim and Manasseh. **Besides Benjamin, Joseph was <u>the youngest</u> son of Jacob.**

In *The "Last Days" Timeline – Volume 1*, it shows that **The Lost 10 Tribes from the North, as the Lion Kingdom,** come to rescue The Church of Jesus Christ, which contain Gentiles of Ephraim, **that are planted into the scriptural roots of Manasseh.**

So the question is, which of the Gentile branches get destroyed first, after the Times of the Gentiles are fulfilled?

The Church of Jesus Christ will be under attack from the Gentiles that have turned away from the message of truth; this is the very definition of **the end** of the Times of the Gentiles. (See Appendix: The Times of the Gentiles)

The Whore Church has mounted on top of the 4th Beast Kingdom of the Gentiles as a new pseudo-state religion.

Thus, the first Gentile branch that gets removed from the Mother Tree is the nation and people that support the attack named The Great Persecution Period.

That will be in America.

They are attacking the Church of Jesus Christ that is home-based in America.

That is the land that will be cleared first, to make way for Israelites to inherit the desolate cities of the Gentiles.

Eventually, the new Nation of Zion will be based in Jackson County Missouri, as its capital city in the heart of America. Wow.

The Ezra's Eagle Prophecy shows the end of the Eagle Kingdom, and it's refreshing or restoration of The U.S. Constitution.

And here is the same concept of the 1st most-wicked Gentile branch being taken off the Mother Tree and burned.

Which **"burning"** is the same language that The Lion does to the wicked Eagle Kingdom.

Only to have the Lion Kingdom of The Lost 10 Tribes return occupancy of Joseph's Promised Land to Ephraim and Manasseh.

Joseph's Promised Land of America is Next-in-Line for Restoration.

Having the next youngest tribe of Israel grafted into their Promised Land to build up something BIG. (Zion)

That is **not the end** of the grafting. It is only the beginning.

The BIG Work Comes Next

The Master/Father has high expectations for His Vineyard. And to make sure the plan is carried out successfully, He is going to need more help. And He gets it.

Next, see what the BIG work looks like in the future to 2019.

18. This Last Work in The Vineyard Is a Big Job – Call For Some Help

After the *Times of the Gentiles* have been fulfilled, **the most bitter Gentile branches are ready to be burned.** Those Gentile nations that cause the most wickedness will be judged by the Father and be taken down and destroyed.

In the future to 2019, there is just such a time and sequence of events to accomplish that judgment of God. The full description of this sequence of events is in the book: *The Last Days Timeline* by James T. Prout (See: www.LastDaysTimeline.com)

The following verses are more instructions from Father to Jesus about **the special helpers** that need to be called during this completion of the Times of the Gentiles takedown period. This is yet future to 2019.

Who Are These Additional Servants?

It has been theorized that this scripture means more missionaries or modern prophets. Let's discover who these additional servants are.

> (Jacob 5:61-63 accents added)
> "**61** Wherefore, go to, and **call servants**, that we may labor diligently with our might in the vineyard, that we may **prepare the way**, that I may **bring forth again the natural fruit**, which natural fruit is good and the **most precious** above all other fruit.

62 Wherefore, let us go to and labor with our might **this last time**, for behold **the end draweth nigh**, and this is for **the last time** that I shall prune my vineyard.

63 Graft in the branches; **begin at the last that they may be first**, and that **the first may be last**, and **dig** about the **trees, both old and young**, the **first and the last**; and **the last and the first**, that **all** may be **nourished** once again for **the last time**."

Learning Points:
- A. The Father/Master/Lord instructs Jesus/The Servant to **call other servants**. It is in Jesus' responsibility to make the judgment on who he will call.
- B. The Natural Fruit – another qualifier was added that the natural fruit was "**most precious above all other fruit.**" So, again the natural fruit is **of great worth** to The Father. It is the very purpose of the whole vineyard. It is the very purpose of The Father's work in the vineyard. The end result.
  - a. What is the desired end result of the work of God with this Earth? Moses 1:39 "For behold, this is my work and my glory—to bring to pass **the immortality and eternal life of man.**"
  - b. The Natural Fruit again is defined as: **adding glory** to The Father by having his children gain immortality and eternal life. Crowned with the abilities and responsibilities of Godhood. Creators of yet still future worlds. Eventually worlds without number.
- C. **The Last Time** – This large call of additional servants to do

the work in the vineyard is the last great missionary effort on this earth before the Millennium. This "Last Missionary Moment", comes **after** the Times of the Gentiles have been fulfilled. This is not a missionary program **during** the Times of the Gentiles. This is shown in coming the verses.

D. **What Are These Servants Called to Do?**: These servants are called to **take-down those Gentiles from off the Mother Tree**. These Gentile branches have become wild over 2000 years of existence on the Mother Tree with the scripture roots since 36-70AD. Also, these additional servants are called to **prune, dig, trim and labor along side The Father and Jesus Christ** in the next few verses.

That sounds like a fantastic job. To labor **along-side** The Father and Jesus Christ. Where do I sign-up?

That intake process will be in the future to 2019.

I imagine that the long Zion's Camp march in the 1830s was a tool to select the 12 Apostles in this last dispensation. So too, the future long march to the New Jerusalem in Jackson County Missouri will be a proving ground for the 144,000. (12,000 of each Tribe of Israel, approximately)

19. How Will The Father Eliminate The Wicked People in The Gentile Nations That Currently Cumber The Ground of His Earth?

What follows is further instructions from Father to Jesus about nourishing the trees and the **manner of removal** of the bad branches.

This next section of the prophecy deals with the new Nation of Zion. Also, it deals with the further removal of non-Believing Gentiles from America, Europe and the rest of the world.

To understand this, one must know who the Gentiles are. (See previous chapter in this work for elaboration)

Ask yourself some hard questions about history to the 2019 time period:
1. Who are the Gentiles specifically?
2. What religious denominations do they carry among them?
3. How did those denominations begin?
4. How did the Gentiles spread around-the-world historically?
5. How will the non-Believing Gentiles meet their end in America in prophecy? (See book: *The Last Days Timeline – Volume 1*)
6. How will the non-Believing Gentiles meet their end in Europe and the rest of the world in prophecy? (See book: *The Last Days Timeline – Volume 1*)

Now, let's read what The Master of the Vineyard will do in reality, relayed through this prophecy.

> (Jacob 5:64-66 accents added)
> "**64** Wherefore, **dig** about them, and **prune** them, and **dung** them **once more, for the last time**, for **the end draweth nigh**. And if it be so that these last grafts shall grow, and bring forth the natural fruit, then shall ye **<u>prepare the way for them</u>**, that they may grow.
> **65** And as **they begin** to grow ye shall **<u>clear away the branches</u>** which bring forth bitter fruit, **according to <u>the strength of the good</u> and the size thereof**; and ye shall **<u>not clear away the bad thereof all at once</u>**, lest **the roots thereof should be <u>too strong</u> for the graft**, and the graft thereof shall perish, and I lose the trees of my vineyard.
> **66** For it grieveth me that I should lose the trees of my vineyard; wherefore ye shall **<u>clear away the bad according as the good shall grow</u>**, that the **root and the top may be equal in strength**, until the good shall overcome the bad, and the bad be hewn down and cast into the **fire**, that they cumber not the ground of my vineyard; and thus will I **sweep away the bad** out of my vineyard."

Learning Points:

A. Dig, Prune, and Dung – These 3 works have already been discussed in an earlier chapter. However, here they are again. These represent a new work for God to do in the Earth with man. The future to 2019 will see God's Hand in much bigger ways working with the nations.

B. The Last Time – There are many mentions of this "last time" in this section of the prophecy. This will be the last great work of God in the Earth before the 1000 year Millennium of Christ.
C. **The End** – As we will see in further verses, this "end" is not when Christ comes, but is the end of the Millennium when the earth passes away and becomes resurrected, then celestialized.
D. How can scripture roots be **too strong** for the people connected to them? (See Author's Analysis section below)
E. **Prepare the Way for Israel to Grow** – When Israel begins to be rejoined into the Mother Tree (the true Church planted in the promised lands), the bad Gentile branches are to be removed slowly to make way for Israel to grow in their stead.
   a. This means that **after** the Fulfillment of the Times of the Gentiles, The Church of Jesus Christ will have land to grow. The same land will be swept clean of the Unbelieving Gentiles. The **Believing Gentiles** as primarily of Ephraim will grow in their stead. This is the creation of the **new Nation of Zion in the Americas**. The center place or capital being **Jackson County Missouri** with the special Temple complex.
   b. As the new Nation of Zion grows, more land will be made available over the whole earth, **slowly - not all at once**, from where the Unbelieving Gentiles currently reside. There will be a delicate balance.
   c. Yet, the last Gentile lands to be made available will be Europe itself, through the 7 Vials and 7 Trumpets of

John the Revelator. (see book: *The Last Days Timeline* by James T. Prout)

F. **According to the Strength of the Good and the Size Thereof** – The Nation of Zion will start small. Yet, will grow in size and maturity of years. Zion is to be a land of security for righteous people all over the world to gather. Against the evil Gentile nations, that will be practicing secret combinations with **super wicked statecraft rulers. Including the Stout Horn Antichrist.**

G. **The Root and Top Shall Be Equal in Strength** – Remember, the problem of the wild Gentile branches was that the "TOP BRANCHES" took power unto themselves and overran the roots/scriptures. This shall not happen again in the Nation of Zion with the 12 Tribes of Israel being grafted back into the Mother Tree.

H. The wicked non-Believing Gentiles are to be swept off the Mother Tree and burned. Notice the words "burn" and the use of "fire". Many prophecies use **this terminology** to describe the end result of the wicked non-believing Gentile nations. (See book: *The Last Days Timeline – Volume 1*)

Author's Analysis:

How can scripture roots be too strong for the people connected to them?

I thought about this a while. I have studied the Book of Mormon. I know that a large portion of the sealed plates contains the writings of The Brother of Jared. Further, these were so powerful that they **destroyed faith**, and brought a person to **a perfect knowledge** of God and how things **really** work.

So, it would be possible that the scriptures could hurt **the faith process of growth** in the people.

Remember, faith is the main **driver of righteous actions** in this world. The pre-mortal spirits in the Celestial Kingdom dwelling with Father in Heaven didn't need much faith. They saw everything as it was.

In the Plan of Salvation, it was this earth-life that we are to have our memory wiped by the Veil of Forgetfulness and live by faith in the Word of God.

Further, IF our Father in Heaven simply cleared ALL the bad Gentile branches and re-grafted all of Israel on the mother tree all at once; this would quickly release **all** the scriptures to **all** the people **all** at the same time. Including the strongest root scriptures to the weakest of the branches. (**Assumingly,** some branches are stronger than others.)

That would be a "shocking" process for the tree and the branches. That big of a shock may kill the entire tree.

Also, there is the issue of **accountability**. Those additional scripture roots would contain **all** the commandments ever

> given by God to mankind. Including Enoch's day, before the Great Flood, when the whole community of the City of Enoch was translated.
>
> Once we have a commandment, we are expected to follow it. That may not be easy for some people who love God, but are immediately weak. Thus, bringing potentially many people under condemnation and sin.
>
> There would be no stair-step rise to God. Line upon line. Precept upon precept. There would be a high-speed elevator. That may be dangerous.
>
> I believe that is what The Master/Father intended with the concept that the scripture roots could overpower the quickly grafted branches.

The *Times of the Gentiles* are now complete. The new Nation of Zion is established. The wicked 4th Beast Kingdom of The Gentiles is on the run in Europe. They are kicked out of America.

The Natural Branches are being planted in the lands of their inheritance, **slowly and surely**…as the Bad Fruit Unbelieving Gentiles are being removed.

20. How Shall They Be "One"?

In the future, the Nation of Zion will be established in the once stronghold of Gentile America.

That new Nation of Zion will be very different than any other nation in the recent 2000 year history of this world. It will derive its roots and culture from a time much older than recorded history.

> (Jacob 5:67-69 accents added)
> "**67** And the branches of the natural tree will I graft in again into the natural tree;
> **68** And the branches of the natural tree will I graft into the natural branches of the tree; and thus will I bring them **together again**, that they shall bring forth **the natural fruit, and <u>they shall be one</u>**.
> **69** And **the bad shall be cast away**, yea, **even out of all the land of my vineyard**; for behold, **only this once** will I prune my vineyard."

Learning Points:

A. They shall be "one" – This **oneness** is strong evidence that this period we are looking at is **the Zion period** in the future to 2019. Under the new Nation of Zion, the **Law of Consecration** will be practiced in full. **It will succeed** in bringing forth the natural fruit in the lives of mankind that The

Father desires. (See: *The "Last Days" Timeline – Volume 1* chapters on Law of Consecration Practiced in Zion)
- B. The bad non-believing Gentile nations are to be taken away and burned, never to be part of the vineyard again.
- C. Only This Once – Again, this Zion period will be the "last time" of God's major work on this Earth. Welcome it when it comes. And see the hand of God work among the nations.

Action: The Servant/Jesus Calls 144,000

The plan for the future is set. Now comes **action**.

During this period of the Nation of Zion, the main prophetic accomplishment is the building of the special temple in Jackson County Missouri. Also the calling of the 144,000 high priests (12,000 from each of the 12 Tribes of Israel, approximately). To be sent forth with special powers to gather righteous people out of each nation and bring them to Zion.

> (Jacob 5:70-72 accents added)
> "**70** And it came to pass that the Lord of the vineyard **sent his servant**; and the servant went and did as the Lord had commanded him, and **brought other servants**; and <u>they were few</u>.
> 71 And <u>the Lord</u> of the vineyard said unto them: Go to, and labor in the vineyard, with your might. For behold, this is **the last time** that I shall **nourish** my vineyard; for **the end is nigh at hand**, and the season speedily cometh; and if ye labor

with your might **with me** ye shall have **joy in the fruit** which I shall lay up unto myself against the time which will soon come. **72** And it came to pass that the **servants** did go and labor with their mights; and the Lord of the vineyard **labored also with them**; and **they did obey the commandments** of the Lord of the vineyard **in all things**."

Learning Points:
- A. The Master/Lord/Father sent The Servant/Jesus to do the work of calling other servants.
- B. **The additional servants.** Are they prophets? Are they missionaries? Or are they the 144,000?
    - a. Prophets – They can't be prophets and be congruent with the storyline of the prophecy. Ancient Israel had prophets. Modern Israel as the Church of Jesus Christ has had prophets since 1830.
        - i. Were there additional servants called at any other time in this prophecy? (no)
        - ii. Are we looking at the last time the Father will do a work in the vineyard? (yes)
        - iii. Are we looking at a period when the fruit will be "one" and the Gentile nations will be burned? (yes)
        - iv. Has that happened yet in 2019? (no)
        - v. Has the Times of The Gentiles been fulfilled yet? (no)

b. <u>Missionaries</u> – They can't be missionaries of the current 1830-2019 time period and be congruent with the storyline of the prophecy for the same reasons above.
c. <u>144,000</u> – Yes, the calling of the 144,000 seems to be congruent with the storyline of the prophecy.
   i. Are the 144,000 special servants called after the Times of the Gentiles have been fulfilled? (yes)
   ii. Are the 144,000 called by Jesus (The Servant) himself in the Nation of Zion period? (yes)
   iii. Do the 144,000 do the pruning, digging, dunging by shaking up the nations and gathering righteous people out from the wicked Gentile nations and the whole earth to store-up precious souls for The Father? (yes)
d. <u>Lion Kingdom</u> – Possibly, there is a 4th option that seems to fit. The Lion Kingdom with John the Revelator that will come from the North including the Lost 10 Tribes of Israel. They will come as the Army of The Lord specifically to take down the Unbelieving Gentiles. (See: *The Last Days Timeline – Volume 1*) So this seems to fit as well. But since the Lost **10** Tribes are going to be a good-sized portion of the 144,000, they seem to be nearly one and the same.

C. They Were Few – This is the part where many people are confused as to who the additional servants are. Are 144,000 a few? Well yes and no. Are they a few compared to the population of the planet? (yes) - Are they a few compared to a few prophets of God? (no) - However, in the storyline of the prophecy, the 144,000 could be considered "a few".

D. The Father will himself give the 144,000 this charge, written above.
E. The Father will work in the vineyard with these additional servants. He is "hands-on" during this period of future history of the world.
F. The additional servants accomplish the mission, obey all the commandments and succeed.

21. It Works! The Nation of Zion Succeeds in Producing Natural Fruit From All 12 of Israel`s Branches. The Unbelieving Gentile Branches Are Removed and Burned.

The Lost 10 Tribes are to return and participate in becoming a large part of the 144,000 servants.

A Zion society is created upon The Law of Consecration in the future to 2019. Of the many times it has been started in the past, this one succeeds to usher in the 1000 year Millennium of Jesus Christ. (See: *The "Last Days" Timeline – Volume 1*)

The landmasses on Earth are cleared of non-Believing Gentiles to encourage the new Nation of Zion to spread her tent and inherit the desolate cities.

>(Jacob 5:73-74 accents added)
>"**73** And there **began** to be the **natural fruit again** in the vineyard; and the **natural branches began to grow and thrive** exceedingly; and the **wild branches began to be plucked off** and to be cast away; and they did keep **the root and the top thereof equal**, according to the strength thereof. **74** And thus **they labored**, with all diligence, according to the commandments of the Lord of the vineyard, **even until the bad had been cast away out of the vineyard**, and the Lord had preserved unto himself the trees which had become **again the natural fruit**; and they became like unto **one body**; and **the**

fruits were equal; and the Lord of the vineyard had preserved unto himself the natural fruit, which was **most precious** unto him from the beginning."

Learning Points:
- A. These 2 verses show a beginning and a near-ending of the work.
- B. As there begins to show natural fruit again, **the first Tribe of Israel branch replaces the first Gentile branch.** Notice again, that the last shall be first. The near-last born of the 12 Tribes of Israel **was Joseph**. And the last born of his 2 sons was Ephraim. **So, Ephraim is to be first to inherit the land from a wild Gentile branch.** We know that the majority of the initial Church of Jesus Christ was of Ephraim, and it nearly stands that way in 2019. So, when the first group comes to Jackson County Missouri to establish the land for the New Jerusalem temple, it will be **Ephraim to be grafted in at the first**. And we know that there will be many more of Israel very soon after that.
  - a. **Author's Analysis:** One could make the case that Ephraim is even planted today, before the demarcation of the Times of the Gentiles being fulfilled.
- C. At the beginning, the natural branches of Israel grow and thrive well. This takes place at the same time that the initial wild Gentile branches are being plucked off and burned.
  - a. **Author's Analysis:** This is a proof point to show that of all the Gentile nations within the last-days 4th Beast Kingdom of the Gentiles, **America will be the first to**

fall. It's all about *the promises on the land.* (See book: *The Last Days Timeline – Volume 1*)

D. The root (scriptures and the word of God) and the branches (the leadership and members of the 12 Tribes of Israel) were kept on-track with The Church of Jesus Christ (The tree trunk).

E. At the ending, we see that the wild fruit Gentile nations that were cumbering the tree were all (100%) cut off from the tree and burned with fire. Their land has been opened up to be inhabited by the new Nation of Zion as it spreads. (See: *The "Last Days" Timeline – Volume 1* for scripture references)

F. One Body and The Fruits Were Equal – Again another reference to the Law of Consecration that shall be practiced successfully during the Nation of Zion period.

G. The goal of The Master/Father is to preserve the precious natural fruit. It was the goal in the beginning and it is still the goal in the future to 2019.

The branches are being moved now. The additional helpers are making it happen. Things are looking good.

22. *The Natural Fruit Has Been Restored – The 144,000 Have Been Successful*

The mission of the 144,000 is to hunt the righteous and pure in heart from among the wicked and gather them to the new Nation of Zion. They succeed in that mission.

Listen to the blessings which will be had by the 144,000 servants.

> (Jacob 5:75 accents added)
> "**75** And it came to pass that when the Lord of the vineyard saw that **his fruit was good**, and that his **vineyard was no more corrupt**, he **called up his servants**, and said unto them: Behold, for **this last time** have **we nourished** my vineyard; and thou beholdest that I have done according to my will; and I have preserved the natural fruit, that it is good, even **like as it was in the beginning**. And blessed art <u>**thou**</u>; for because ye have been diligent in laboring with me in my vineyard, and have kept my commandments, and have brought unto me again the natural fruit, that my vineyard is no more corrupted, and the bad is cast away, behold <u>**ye shall have joy with me**</u> because of the fruit of my vineyard."

Learning Points:
   A. This verse is the ending of the mission of the 144,000. They are successful.

B. The natural fruit is had in great abundance once again. The natural good fruit is just as it was in Israel in the beginning.
   a. **Author's Analysis**: I have read claims that this fruit of the beginning was actually the good fruit of the Zion society of Enoch. However, since this prophecy opens when the nations of Northern Israel and Southern Judah are in decay, it reasons, that we are talking about the beginning of the natural branches of Israel.
C. The blessings upon the 144,000 are that they will have joy with The Father and The Saints in the Kingdom of God. This would also imply that **their Calling and Election is made sure** by the mouth of God the Father Himself.

The 144,000 have received their reward. All looks good. Why hasn't the Prophecy of the Wild and Tame Olive Trees finished up yet?

23. The Great 1000 Year Millennium Appears Before Us

After the wild Gentile nations have been cut off and burned, the 12 Tribes of Israel have brought forth good natural fruit again.

Now The Father will continue to collect this good fruit "for a long time".

> (Jacob 5:76 accents added)
>
> "**76** For behold, **for a long time** will I **lay up of the fruit** of my vineyard unto mine own self **against the season**, which speedily cometh; and for **the last time** have I **nourished** my vineyard, and **pruned** it, and **dug** about it, and **dunged** it; wherefore I will lay up unto mine own self of the fruit, **for a long time**, according to that which I have spoken."

Learning Points:

A. This "long time" that The Father will lay up good fruit is the **1000 year Millennium of Christ.** During this time period the Zion society will flourish and continue to produce good obedient repentant people without the influence of Lucifer. **Much glory will be added to The Father** during this time period.

B. Note: The final season **is not yet**.

C. Nourished, pruned, dug, dunged already happened – It appears that The Father will have **less activity** in this hands-off period during the Millennium.

a. **Author's Analysis:** Presumably, this will be when Jesus, as The Servant, will be in the Vineyard doing the normal harvesting of the good fruit for The Father.

The 1000 year Millennium of Jesus Christ is the time for the best Good Fruit production in the Vineyard.

This is the time period when man advances faster than all the 6000 years of the past.

But, are their trials during the Millennium? (yes)

The biggest trial for those sons and daughters of God born during the Millennium will be **at the end**. They will get their trial during the last battle; when Lucifer will be loosed upon the world once more.

24. The End of The Millennium – More Bad Fruit

At the end of the Earth, there will come a time period when Lucifer is released from his shackles and will once again tempt mankind.

This will produce **bad fruit**. People that will fight against God.

Also, after this final moment with the Battle of Gog and Magog, Lucifer's armies lose and are burned by fire from the heavens. The righteous are saved, once again by the arm of God.

The Earth herself dies and is Celestialized in eternal burnings.

> (Jacob 5:77 accents added)
> "**77** And when the time cometh that **evil fruit shall again come** into my vineyard, **then** will I cause **the good and the bad to be gathered**; and the good will I preserve unto myself, and **the bad will I cast away into its own place**. And **then cometh the season and the end**; and **my vineyard will I cause to be burned** with fire."

Learning Points:
  A. At the end of this "long time" of the 1000 year Millennium, more evil bad fruit arises…**on its own**. There were no more transplants this time.
  B. The Good Fruit is gathered up and the Bad Fruit is gathered as well.

C. The good righteous followers of God are preserved at the end of the Millennium. The Bad Fruit are cast into "their place."
   a. **Author's Analysis:** This could mean "outer darkness", or it could mean "hell" to suffer for their own sins. However, since we know that Hell closes its doors at the end of the Millennium and the Final Judgment happens at that time; it is highly likely that these sinful people at the end of the Millennium **have turned from great light and are rebelling and fighting against God on-purpose.** Thus, they are the definition of The Sons of Perdition.
D. **Burning the Vineyard** – The prophecy says that at the end of the growing season, there is **a burning**. This would represent when the earth herself dies and is resurrected into eternal burnings as a celestial kingdom. At this point, the Father comes to dwell on this earth for a time.

Lucifer is Bound During the Millennium – Until The End…

This material is found in the Book of John's Revelation, at the end.

(Rev 20:1-3 accents added)
"**1** And I saw an angel come down from heaven, having the key of the bottomless pit and **a great chain in his hand.**
2 And he <u>**laid hold on**</u> the **dragon**, that **old serpent**, which is the **Devil**, and **Satan**, and bound him <u>**a thousand years**</u>,
3 And **cast him** into the bottomless pit, and **shut him up**, and **set a seal upon him**, that he should deceive the nations no

more, **till the thousand years should be fulfilled**: and after that he **must be loosed a little season**."

Learning Points:
A. Lucifer (or Satan) is **bound** and **cast into a pit** with **a seal** put upon him. He will not be doing any evil deceptions upon mankind for 1000 years.
   a. **Author's Analysis**: I have read and heard it said that during the Millennium that the people will be so righteous that they won't listen to Lucifer anymore. These types of words like "**bound**," "**cast into a pit**," and "**a seal placed upon him**" don't sound like Lucifer is going to be ABLE to do anything for 1000 years. It sounds like he is imprisoned in a pit. **Not** that the people have become so righteous,...and that Lucifer was left alone to tempt man.
B. **A little season** – A little season at the end of the Millennium to once again tempt and ensnare mankind. Make up your mind now, to be on God's side of that battle. It will fool many souls born during the Millennium.

Now, see the final Battle that Lucifer will unleash upon the Millennial inhabitants of earth, while it is in a Terrestrial sphere.

The Battle of The Great God - The Battle of Gog and Magog

This is the last battle on this earth ever to be fought. There will be no more.

However, with the anticipated population explosion during the 1000 year Millennium of Christ, the battle itself will be epic. The largest ever fought.

Even bigger than the Battle of Armageddon, just **prior to** the Millennium.

> (Rev 20:7-9 accents added)
> "7 And **when the thousand years are expired, Satan shall be loosed out of <u>his prison</u>**,
> 8 And shall go out **to deceive the nations** which are in the four quarters of the earth, <u>**Gog and Magog**</u>, to **gather them together to battle**: the number of whom is as **<u>the sand of the sea.</u>**
> 9 And they went up on the breadth of the earth, and **compassed the camp of the saints** about, **and the beloved city**: and <u>**fire came down**</u> from God out of heaven, and devoured them."

Learning Points:
  A. Lucifer is loosed from his **<u>prison</u>**. There is that concept again of a prison.
  B. **The Battle of Gog and Magog** – This is it. The biggest battle ever to happen on the earth. The hosts of war are as the sand

of the sea. Since we are dealing with a time period where there are resurrected bodies and regular mortal bodies, there may be a mix. However, resurrected bodies cannot die a 2nd time. So, this one will be interesting to see how it plays out.

C. **The battle is quick** – apparently there is much time and effort spent on Lucifer's behalf to gather large numbers of people to circle around the city of God which has the camp of the Saints nearby. However, when the battle is to take place, God simply wipes them all out via fire from the sky. They are done.

This concludes the Prophecy of the Wild and Tame Olive Trees. The fruit of glory has been gathered to The Father.

The purpose of this earth has been accomplished. The Vineyard of this earth may now enter into her celestial rest.

25. How Can I Use This Information To Prepare My Family?

When there are tough times ahead, it is always important to remember this Prophecy of The Tame and Wild Olive Trees.

This prophecy will allow you to know that God is in control. All of these writings of Zenos were had thousands of years ago.

This plan is being enacted on the stage of world history right now…and all the way through the end of the Millennium of Christ.

This book is meant to show that this prophecy alone is so detailed that it **was not** and **could not** be written by a 20 something-year-old farm boy named Joseph Smith Jr.

This prophecy was written by Zenos as a prophet of God and recorded a 2nd time, in full detail within our Book of Mormon.

Stand by the church that stands by **the book** that contains this advanced prophecy.

Have faith that you are **a believing Gentile**. (if you aren't native-born of Israel, of course)

Have faith that you are in the right place…in the Old Ship Zion. Endure to the end performing righteousness with your family.

If you happen to be a reader that is not yet a member of The Church of Jesus Christ of Latter-day Saints; seek out and talk with the Missionaries of the church.

I was shown how to feel the spirit by my first missionary before I was baptized. Then 18 months later, I served a mission and gave that gift to many others.

There will come a large event in the future, when the new Nation of Zion is forming that will alert everyone that there is something special going on.

But, don't wait till then to learn about Jesus Christ's true church on the earth. The roots and the tree are here. The first few grafts of branches have already taken place. Take action today. For your special scriptural rootstock is The Book of Mormon.

Your future glory depends upon it. Become a "good fruit."

This End…is only your beginning.

Original Artwork

Appendix 1: The Teachings of Zenos

This appendix section is to give an overview of the doctrines taught by Zenos as recorded by the prophet/writers in the Book of Mormon.

Going straight through the Book of Mormon:

- 1 Nephi 19:10-12 - Zenos prophesied of Jesus Christ's 3 days in the tomb.

- 1 Nephi 19:16 – Zenos is seeing the future gathering of all the tribes of Israel. Remember, he recorded the Prophecy of the Tame and Wild Olive Trees. So he knows that will one day happen.

- Alma 33: 2-11 – Zenos is teaching proper prayer toward God. Zenos was spoken of by Alma the Younger as he was preaching to the lowly Zoramites.

- Alma 34:7 – Zenos teaches about the Son of God. In his day pre-600 B.C. this may be looked upon as blasphemy by Israel. Yet, not only that, but Zenos teaches that The Son is how Israel is to be redeemed. Not the Law of Moses.

- Helaman 8:19 – Zenos was killed for his testimony of Jesus

- Helaman 15:11 – There is an inference that Zenos knew that the Lamanites would in the future be restored to the Gospel. Remember, this information is ultimately coming from the Prophecy of The Tame and Wild Olive Trees.

- 3 Nephi 10:15 - Testified of the destruction at Christ's death. And since the old world wasn't destroyed, I can only affirm that Zenos saw the New World's destruction.

When Did Zenos Live?

He was in the Old Testament and was a great prophet. His information was recorded on the Brass Plates.

This means Zenos lived prior to 600 B.C. when Nephi and Lehi lived. Let's narrow it down a little bit:

- Was Zenos after the flood – yes most probably.
- Was Zenos after Abraham, Isaac, and Jacob. Yes, or he would have been a father of nations.

- Was he after Moses? YES because he speaks of the houses of Israel being led away. And the first of these happened when The 10 Tribes of Northern Israel were led away.
- What prophets would Zenos had been a contemporary?
    - **Author's Analysis**: It appears we are discussing **future items** to the Northern Kingdom of Israel being carried away into Assyria (740 B.C.), during the Prophecy of The Tame and Wild Olive Trees. So most likely Zenos is preaching from 930 B.C. to 722 B.C.. This means that Zenos may be a **contemporary with Elijah, Elisha, Joel, Amos, Isaiah, Micah, or Hosea.**

Zenos will be an amazing scriptural read in the future, when the fullness of his record is revealed. I am eager to read his message.

Appendix 2: Recognizing The Great Apostasy

Martin Luther

(public domain image)

You may already know the story of Martin Luther (1483-1546 A.D.) That he was a German priest that got upset about the Roman Catholic Church and nailed his 95 Theses to the church door in 1517 A.D.

What you may not know at the time was that Martin Luther was a German that was living in the Holy Roman Empire, which was neither holy nor Roman. It was the area we call Germany today.

With Martin Luther's excommunication by the Pope at the Diet of Worms in 1521, he was now **an outlaw** of the Holy Roman Empire/Germany which is where he lived.

These 95 Theses occurred <u>after</u> Luther's trip to Rome itself. He saw things there that shook him up as a man of faith. Rome, the center of the faith was far different than he had been told about or was expecting.

Here are the 95 Theses that show the beginning of the Protest Movement, or Protestant Movement. Notice that **all of them** are calling attention to **a doctrinal shift** away from what the Apostles of Jesus Christ taught in the Bible:

> (*The Ninety-Five Theses* by Martin Luther, also called *Disputation on the Power and Efficacy of Indulgences*)
> "1. When our Lord and Master, Jesus Christ, said "Repent," He called for the entire life of believers to be one of **penitence**.
>
> 2. The **word cannot be properly understood** as referring the sacrament of penance, i.e., confession and satisfaction, as administered by the clergy.
>
> 3. Yet its meaning is not restricted to penitence in one's heart; for such penitence is **null unless it produces outwards signs** in various mortifications of the flesh.
>
> 4. As long as hatred of self abides (i.e., true inward penitence) the penalty of sin abides, viz., until we enter the kingdom of heaven.
>
> 5. The **pope has neither the will nor the power to remit any penalties** beyond those imposed either at his own discretion or by canon law.

6. The **pope himself cannot remit guilt**, but only declare and confirm that it has been remitted by God; or, at most, he can remit it in cases reserved to his discretion. Except for these cases, the guilt remains untouched.

7. God never remits guilt to anyone without, at the same time, making him humbly submissive to the priest, His representative.

8. The penitential canons **apply only to men who are still alive**, and, according to the canons themselves, **none applies to the dead.**

9. Accordingly, the Holy Spirit, acting in the person of the pope, manifests grace to us, by the fact that the **papal regulations always cease to apply at death**, or in any hard case.

10. It is a wrongful act, due to ignorance, when priests retain the canonical **penalties on the dead in purgatory**.

11. When **canonical penalties were changed and made to apply to purgatory**, surely it would seem that tares were sown while the bishops were asleep.

12. In former days, the canonical penalties were imposed, **not after, but before absolution** was pronounced; and were intended to be tests of true contrition.

13. **Death puts an end to all the claims of the church**; even the dying are already dead to the canon laws, and are no longer bound by them.

14. Defective piety or love in a dying person is necessarily accompanied by great fear, which is greatest where the piety or love is least.

15. This **fear or horror is sufficient in itself, whatever else might be said, to constitute the pain of purgatory**, since it approaches very closely to the horror of despair.

16. There seems to be **the same difference between hell, purgatory**, and heaven as between despair, uncertainty, and assurance.

17. Of a truth, **the pains of souls in purgatory ought to be abated**, and charity ought to be proportionately increased.

18. Moreover, it does not seem proved, on any grounds of reason or Scripture, that these souls are outside the state of merit, or unable to grow in grace;

19. Nor does it seem proved to be always the case that they are certain and assured of salvation, even if we are very certain of it ourselves.

20. Therefore the pope, in speaking of the plenary remission of all penalties, does not mean "all" in the strict sense, but only those imposed by himself.

21. Hence **those who preach indulgences are in error** when they say that a man is absolved and saved from every penalty by the pope's indulgences;

22. Indeed, **he cannot remit to souls in purgatory any penalty** which canon law declares should be suffered in the present life.

23. If plenary remission could be granted to anyone at all, it would be only in the cases of the most perfect, i.e., to very few.

24. It must therefore be the case **that the major part of the people are deceived** by that indiscriminate and highsounding promise of relief from penalty.

25. The same power as the pope exercises in general over purgatory is exercised in particular by every single bishop in his bishopric and priest in his parish.

26. The pope does excellently when he grants remission to the souls in purgatory on account of intercessions made on their behalf, and not by the power of the keys (which he cannot exercise for them).

27. There is no divine authority for preaching that the soul flies out of purgatory immediately the money clinks in the bottom of the chest.

28. It is certainly possible that when the money clinks in the bottom of the chest avarice and greed increase; but when the church offers intercession, all depends on the will of God.

29. Who knows whether all souls in purgatory wish to be redeemed in view of what is said of St. Severinus and St. Paschal?2

30. No one is sure of the reality of his own contrition, much less of receiving plenary forgiveness.

31. **One who in good faith** buys indulgences is as rare as a truly penitent man, i.e., very rare indeed.

32. All those who believe themselves certain of their own **salvation by means of letters of indulgence**, will be eternally damned, together with their teachers.

33. We should be most carefully on our guard against those who say that **the papal indulgences are an inestimable divine gift, and that a man is reconciled to God by them.**

34. For the grace conveyed by these indulgences relates simply to the penalties of the sacramental "satisfactions"

decreed merely by man. 35. It is not in accordance with Christian doctrine to preach and teach that those who buy off souls, or purchase confessional licenses, have no need to repent of their own sins.

36. Any Christian whatsoever, who is truly repentant, enjoys plenary remission from penalty and guilt and this is given him without letters of indulgence.

37. Any true Christian whatsoever, living or dead, participates in all the benefits of Christ and the Church; and this participation is granted to him by God without letters of indulgence.

38. Yet the pope's remission and dispensation are in no way to be despised, for, as already said, they proclaim the divine remission.

39. It is very difficult, even for the most learned theologians, to extol to the people the great bounty contained in the indulgences, while, at the same time, praising contrition as a virtue.

40. A truly contrite sinner seeks out, and loves to pay, the penalties of his sins; whereas the very multitude of indulgences dulls men's consciences, and tends to make them hate the penalties.

41 Papal indulgences should only be preached with caution; lest people gain a wrong understanding, and think that they are preferable to other works: those of love.

42. Christians should be taught that the pope does not at all intend that the purchase of indulgences should be understood as at all comparable with works of mercy.

43. **Christians should be taught that one who gives to the poor, or lends to the needy, does a better action than if he purchases indulgences;**

44. Because, by works of love, love grows and a man becomes a better man; whereas, by indulgences, he does not become a better man, but only escapes certain penalties.

45. Christians should be taught that he who sees a needy person, but passes him by although he gives money for indulgences, gains no benefit from the pope's pardon, but only incurs the wrath of God.

46. Christians should be taught that, unless they have more than they need, they are bound to retain what is necessary for the upkeep of their home, and should in no way squander it on indulgences.

47. Christians should be taught that **they purchase indulgences voluntarily**, and are __not under obligation__ to do so.

48. Christians should be taught that, in granting indulgences, the pope has more need, and more desire, for devout prayer on his own behalf than for ready money.

49. Christians should be taught that the pope's indulgences are useful only if one does not rely on them, but most harmful if one loses the fear of God through them.

50. Christians should be taught that, if the pope knew the exactions of the indulgence-preachers, he would rather the church of St. Peter were reduced to ashes than be built with the skin, flesh, and bones of his sheep.

51. Christians should be taught that the pope would be willing, as he ought if necessity should arise, to sell the church of St. Peter, and give, too, his own money to many of those from whom the pardon-merchants conjure money.

52. It is vain to __rely on salvation by letters of indulgence__, even if the commissary, or indeed the pope himself, were to pledge his own soul for their validity.

53. Those are enemies of Christ and the pope who forbid the word of God to be preached at all in some churches, in order that indulgences may be preached in others.

54. The word of God suffers injury if, in the same sermon, an equal or longer time is devoted to indulgences than to that word.

55. The pope cannot help taking the view that if indulgences (very small matters) are celebrated by one bell, one pageant, or one ceremony, the gospel (a very great matter) should be preached to the accompaniment of a hundred bells, a hundred processions, a hundred ceremonies.

56. The treasures of the church, out of which the pope dispenses indulgences, are not sufficiently spoken of or known among the people of Christ.

57. That these treasures are not temporal is clear from the fact that many of the merchants do not grant them freely, but only collect them;

58. Nor are they the merits of Christ and the saints, because even apart from the pope, these merits are always working grace in the inner man, and working the cross, death, and hell in the outer man.

59. St. Laurence said that the poor were the treasures of the church, but he used the term in accordance with the custom of his own time.

60. We do not speak rashly in saying that the treasures of the church are the keys of the church, and are bestowed by the merits of Christ;

61. For it is clear that the power of the pope suffices, by itself, for the remission of penalties and reserved cases.

62. The **true treasure of the church is the Holy Gospel** of the glory and the grace of God,

63. It is right to regard **this treasure as most odious**, for it makes the first to be the last.

64. On the other hand, the treasure of indulgences is most acceptable, for it makes the last to be the first.

65. Therefore the treasures of the gospel are nets which, in former times, they used to fish for men of wealth.

66. The **treasures of the indulgences are the nets today** which they use to fish for men of wealth.

67. The indulgences, which the merchants extol as the greatest of favors, are seen to be, in fact, a favorite means for money-getting;

68. Nevertheless, they are not to be compared with the grace of God and the compassion shown in the Cross.

69. Bishops and curates, in duty bound, must receive the commissaries of the papal indulgences with all reverence;

70. But they are under a much greater obligation to watch closely and attend carefully **lest these men preach their own fancies instead of what the pope commissioned**.

71. Let him be anathema and accursed who denies the apostolic character of the indulgences;

72. On the other hand, let him be blessed who is on his guard against the wantonness and license of the pardon-merchants' words.

73. In the same way, the pope rightly excommunicates those who make any plans to the detriment of the trade in indulgences.

74. It is much more in keeping with his views to excommunicate those who use the pretext of indulgences to plot anything to the detriment of holy love and truth.

75. It **is foolish to think that papal indulgences have so much power that they can absolve a man even if he has done the impossible and violated the mother of God**.

76. We assert the contrary, and say that the pope's pardons are not able to remove the least venial of sins as far as their guilt is concerned.

77. When it is said that not even St. Peter, if he were now pope, could grant a greater grace, it is blasphemy against St. Peter and the pope.

78. We assert the contrary, and say that he, and any pope whatever, possesses greater graces, viz., the gospel, spiritual powers, gifts of healing, etc., as is declared in I Corinthians 12.

79. It is **blasphemy to say that the insignia of the cross with the papal arms are of equal value to the cross on which Christ died.**

80. The bishops, curates, and theologians, who permit assertions of that kind to be made to the people without let or hindrance, will have to answer for it.

81. This unbridled preaching of indulgences makes it difficult for learned men to guard the respect due to the pope against false accusations, or at least from the keen criticisms of the laity;

82. They ask, e.g.: Why does not the pope liberate everyone from purgatory for the sake of love (a most holy thing) and because of the supreme necessity of their souls? This would be morally the best of all reasons. Meanwhile he redeems

innumerable souls for money, a most perishable thing, with which to build St. Peter's church, a very minor purpose.

83. Again: Why should funeral and anniversary masses for the dead continue to be said? And why does not the pope repay, or permit to be repaid, the benefactions instituted for those purposes, since it is wrong to pray for those souls who are now redeemed?

84. Again: Surely this is a new sort of compassion, on the part of God and the pope, when an impious man, an enemy of God, is allowed to pay money to redeem a devout soul, a friend of God; while yet that devout and beloved soul is not allowed to be redeemed without payment, for love's sake, and just because of its need of redemption.

85. Again: Why are the penitential canon laws, which in fact, if not in practice, have long been observed and dead in themselves, — why are they, today, still used in imposing fines in money, through the granting of indulgences, as if all the penitential canons were fully operative?

86. Again: **Since the pope's income to-day is larger than that of the wealthiest of wealthy men**, why does he not build this one church of St. Peter with his own money, rather than with the money of indigent believers?

87. Again: What does the pope remit or dispense to people who, by their perfect penitence, have a right to plenary remission or dispensation?

88. Again: Surely greater good could be done to the church if the pope were to bestow these remissions and dispensations, not once, as now, but a hundred times a day, for the benefit of any believer whatever.

89. What the pope seeks by indulgences is not money, but rather the salvation of souls; why then does he not suspend the letters and indulgences formerly conceded, and still as efficacious as ever?

90. These questions are serious matters of conscience to the laity. To suppress them by force alone, and not to refute them by giving reasons, is to expose the church and the pope to the ridicule of their enemies, and to make Christian people unhappy.

91. If, therefore, indulgences were preached in accordance with the spirit and mind of the pope, all these difficulties would be easily overcome, and, indeed, cease to exist.

92. Away, then, with those prophets who say to Christ's people, "Peace, peace," where there is no peace.

93. Hail, hail to all those prophets who say to Christ's people, "The cross, the cross," where there is no cross.

94. Christians should be exhorted to be zealous to follow Christ, their Head, through penalties, deaths, and hells;

95. And let them thus be more confident of entering heaven through many tribulations rather than through a false assurance of peace."

In Martin Luther's day of the 1520s, the main Christian Church of the day was **collecting the wealth of Europe** through the sale of indulgences to sin.

Note: the ability to sin without earthly penalty has been at the center of all secret combinations since the world began.

William Tyndale

William Tyndale (1494-1536) was the main author of 90-95% of the King James Version of the Bible.

Most of the 1611 King James Version of the Bible used William Tyndale's work and checked it against the Great Bible. Many say that the staff of King James used the original sources, but then referred to Tyndale to check their work. Thus, William Tyndale was the main translator of the Bible we have today.

Tyndale was the primary English Bible translator from the original Greek and Hebrew sources. So, any quotes from him would be related to that work.

> (Selection from *The Obedience of a Christian Man* by William Tyndale)
> "Finally, that this threatening and **forbidding the lay people to read the scripture** is not for the love of your souls (which they care for as the **fox doth for the geese**), is evident, and clearer than the sun; inasmuch as they permit and suffer you to read Robin Hood, and Bevis of Hampton, Hercules, Hector and Troilus, with a thousand histories and fables of love and wantonness, and of ribaldry, as filthy as heart can think, **to corrupt the minds of youth** withal, clean contrary to the doctrine of Christ and of his Apostles: for Paul saith, "See that fornication, and all uncleanness, or covetousness, be not once named among you, as it becometh saints; neither filthiness,

neither foolish talking nor jesting, which are not comely: for this ye know, that no whoremonger, either unclean person, or covetous person, which is the worshipper of images, hath any inheritance in the kingdom of Christ and of God.' And after saith he, 'Through such things cometh the wrath of God upon the children of unbelief.' Now seeing **they permit you freely to read those things which <u>corrupt your minds</u>** and rob you of the kingdom of God and Christ, and bring the wrath of God upon you, how is this forbidding for love of your souls?"

Learning Points:
  A. William Tyndale believed that for the English to feed the youth stories and tales of disdain, that it was **<u>corrupting the mind</u>** of the young. Scripture from God should be the main reading instrument for the youth.
  B. The **forbidding of God's Scripture in the English language as a tool for the layperson**, Tyndale saw as the culprit and the ability to corrupt the minds of the young. **The controlling influence.**
  C. There is the word "corruption" again. Just as in the fruit was corrupted in the Vineyard.

William Tyndale is one of my favorite stories of principled action. The success of Tyndale to change the world is a story for all ages and people's

The best documentary on William Tyndale was done by BYU and is called *Fires of Faith*. (https://www.lastdaystimeline.com/fires-of-faith)

John Calvin

John Calvin 1509-1564 was a French lawyer. He had a gift in verbal-linguistic skills. He wrote a ton of books.

While studying law as a Roman Catholic, The Bible was a mandatory study topic. During this time he was talking with other people who were more humanist in their religious views. This is when Calvin had his first conversion mindset to Protestantism. (See: https://en.wikipedia.org/wiki/John_Calvin)

Later, Calvin had a hand in the Geneva Bible, which was the most used English translation of the Bible until the Authorized King James Version of the Bible was created in 1611. Until then, most English speaking Protestants used the Geneva Bible. John Calvin had put many aggressive footnotes into the Bible. When the Puritans came to America in the early 1600s on the Mayflower and otherwise, the Geneva Bible with John Calvin's footnotes is the Bible they used. (See: https://en.wikipedia.org/wiki/Geneva_Bible)

John Calvin was a fire in his sermons and his pen was venomous. As also shown by these quotes:

(*Antidote to the Council of Trent* (Tracts III:264) by John Calvin)
"Although the devil has long reigned in the Papacy, yet he could not altogether extinguish God's grace: nay, a church is among them."

And...

"The Papacy...has nothing in common with the **ancient form** of the Church."

"I deny that See to be **apostolical**, wherein **nought is seen but a shocking apostasy**."

Those are pretty pointed descriptions. I think John Calvin could say a lot more. But, one thing is for sure...John Calvin saw the Great Apostasy in the 1530s.

Roger Williams

Roger Williams (1603-1683) of the American colonies was the greatest religious leader living in the colonies at that time. But he didn't start out that way.

The Early Days

public domain image

Williams was born in London England in 1603. He went to school to become a Church of England priest. Yet, he joined the Separatist Puritan movement at Cambridge and became a lowly chaplain to Sir William Masham.

Williams did not join the 1st wave of migrations to the Americas with the Puritans on the Mayflower (1620 A.D.). He came over a little later in 1630 A.D. on the Lyon. Williams settled in Boston, Massachusetts.

However, Williams' preaching in the Massachusetts Bay area found that its leaders were not sufficiently separated from The Church of England. (see: https://en.wikipedia.org/wiki/Roger_Williams) They found Williams a heretic. That was fine with Williams.

The Discovery of Important Principles

So, Williams and a few others moved to greener pastures. They settled the area of Providence, Rhode Island; for **he felt that the Providence of God was helping him**. Providence was <u>the first place</u> in all the colonies and the world, where religion was separate from civil government matters. There was **NO STATE RELIGION** in Providence. Also, the principle of **majority rule voting** was implemented.

Roger Williams developed **friendly relations with the American Indians** in the area and bought land from them twice. This was a very different tact from other colonial settlements, then and in the future. Williams believed that the King of England had no right to grant title to Indian lands without their permission, or paying for them. This was the heretic doctrine that got him pushed out of the Massachusetts Bay Colony.

public domain image

He believed the Native Americans **were people**. Not only that, but Williams published **the first** language study of the Native Americans. He mainly studied the language of the Algonquian tribes. (See: https://en.wikipedia.org/wiki/A_Key_Into_the_Language_of_America)

However, Williams did not want to preach Christianity to the Native Americans, for he couldn't speak their language good enough to help them understand Jesus Christ in all of his glory. Williams had great respect for Christ and for other people's rights, and their understanding of conscious.

public domain image

What the Gentiles Did With The Bible After Arriving in The Promised Land

From there, Williams built up his following as true Separatists, in his own view and understanding of the Holy Scriptures which all Puritans **had carried with them over the Atlantic Ocean.**

Roger Williams is one of the best examples of a very early Gentile pioneer who humbled himself before the Lord and succeeded.

(1st Nephi 13:12-20 accents added)

"**13** And it came to pass that I beheld the Spirit of God, that it wrought upon <u>other</u> Gentiles; and **they went forth out of captivity,** upon **the many waters.**

14 And it came to pass that I beheld **many multitudes of the Gentiles** upon the **land of promise**; and I beheld the wrath of God, that it was upon the seed of my brethren; and they were scattered before the Gentiles and were smitten.

15 And I beheld the Spirit of the Lord, that it was upon the Gentiles, and **they did prosper and obtain the bland for their inheritance**; and I beheld that they were white, and exceedingly fair and beautiful, like unto my people before they were slain.

16 And it came to pass that I, Nephi, beheld that the Gentiles who had gone forth out of captivity **did humble themselves** before the Lord; and **the power of the Lord was with them.**"

See what happened to Williams next…

In 1638, Ezekiel Holliman a layperson, not of an official priesthood; baptized Roger Williams into the new Baptist Church. Williams and friend John Clarke established the First Baptist Church in Rhode Island. **They became <u>the founders</u> of the Baptist faith in America.**

The Great Apostasy Acknowledged in Very Early America

What did Roger Williams, the founder of the Baptist faith in America say about Christ's **original church** as established by the 12 Apostles?

> (Picturesque America, or the Land We Live In, ed. William Cullen Bryant, 1872 edition, vol. 1 page 502)
> "...**no regularly-constituted church on earth, nor any person authorized** to administer any Church ordinance; no could there be until, **new Apostles** are sent by the great Head of the Church, for whose coming, **he is seeking**."

But that was not all that Roger Williams said...

> (Struggles and Triumphs of Religious Liberty, by Underhill and Edward, page 238)
> "The **apostasy**... hath so far **corrupted all**, that there can be **no recovery** out of that apostasy until Christ shall send forth **new Apostles to plant churches anew**."

Learning Points:
  A. It appears from these 2 quotes that Roger Williams knew of The Great Apostasy. There is that **"corrupted"** word again. Like the corrupted fruit of the vineyard. An apostasy corrupts.
  B. It appears that Williams recognized that there was no authority from God upon the earth to do any normal church ordinance, including baptism.
  C. It further appears that Williams knew that the original Church of Jesus Christ as written about in the New Testament that had Apostles and Prophets was not around in the 1640s A.D.

D. Roger Williams was **waiting for Christ to restore his church** upon the earth. Which came later in 1830 A.D. through the Prophet Joseph Smith Jr.
E. And with that new church foundation, Roger Williams was waiting for new Apostles to be called and instituted. Which did take place after Joseph Smith's return from the Zion's Camp March in 1835 A.D.

The Foundation Was Laid

Roger Williams founder of the Baptist Church in America was about 200 years ahead of the time he was looking toward.

As modern Latter-day Saints look back to all the good work that Roger Williams had accomplished, it would be hard to say that the restoration of the Gospel of Jesus Christ could be accomplished without the foundation laid by Roger Williams. **He was essential.**

The religious freedom of a separation of church and state **documented first** at the Providence Rhode Island settlement by Roger Williams was to be the #1 foundational doctrine of the U.S. Constitution's **Bill of Rights**.

> (The 1st of the Bill of Rights – The first 10 amendments to the new U.S. Constitution September 25, 1789)
> "**Congress shall make no law respecting an establishment of religion or prohibiting the free exercise thereof**, or abridging the **freedom of speech** or of **the press**, or the

right of the people peaceably to assemble and **to petition the government for a redress** of grievances."

The **Federalist** framers of the Constitution would help the **Anti-Federalist** detractors from The Constitution by promising a Bill of Rights in the 1st congressional session. The Anti-Federalists in the new State houses would not sign the Constitution unless a Bill of Rights was specifically added.

Roger Williams' doctrine of **NO STATE RELIGION** was specifically **the #1 God-given natural right** mentioned in the entire Bill of Rights. The freedom of religion was **ahead of** the right to bear arms, the right against unreasonable searches and seizures, protection of life-liberty-property, and the right to a jury trial. It was THAT important.

This nationally codified freedom of religion was the first of its kind in the world through the U.S. Constitution of 1789. This paved the way, **just barely**, for the newly established Church of Jesus Christ to be birthed in 1830 A.D. and survive. And it had to eventually leave the confines of the United States to endure and grow. And grow it did.

I believe Roger Williams of the 1640s would have been proud of **the use** of the freedoms that he first founded.

A Modern Apostle Looks To The Man... That First Looked To Him

Duly ordained modern Apostle of Jesus Christ Jeffrey R. Holland is a direct-line descendant of Roger Williams. Williams is Elder Holland's 10th Great Grandfather.

In general conference October 2004, in an address titled "Prophets, Seers, and Revelators" Elder Jeffrey R. Holland said these words about his own Great Grandfather:

> (https://www.churchofjesuschrist.org/study/general-conference/2004/10/prophets-seers-and-revelators?lang=eng)
> "Well, Sister Clements, your very tender note recalled for me a **similar hope** and almost the same language **once used in my own family**. In the tumultuous years of the first settlements in this nation, **Roger Williams, my volatile and determined 10th great-grandfather**, fled—not entirely of his own volition—from the Massachusetts Bay Colony and settled in what is now the state of Rhode Island.
>
> He called his headquarters **Providence, the very name itself revealing his lifelong quest for divine interventions and heavenly manifestations**. But he never found what he felt was the true New Testament church of earlier times. Of this disappointed seeker the legendary Cotton Mather said, "Mr. Williams [finally] told [his followers] 'that being himself misled, he had [misled them,'] and] **he was now satisfied that there was none** upon earth that could administer baptism [or any

of the ordinances of the gospel], ... [so] he advised them therefore to *forego* all ... and wait for the coming of *new* Apostles."

Roger Williams did not live to see those longed-for new Apostles raised up, but **in a future time I hope to be able to tell him personally that his posterity did live to see such."**

With ordained Apostles of Jesus Christ now on the Earth, do what Roger Williams implored his congregation to do. Go toward the new Apostles of Jesus Christ with the President of The Church of Jesus Christ of Latter-day Saints at their head. Listen to what they teach and continue to become the Saints of Jesus Christ.

As seekers of truth and members of Christ's Church, we are indebted to the wise American founders **to find** principles of truth and uphold them in our daily lives.

John Wesley

John Wesley (1703 – 1791) led a revival movement inside the Church of England. This movement eventually was called the Methodist Movement.

Originally an Anglican Church of England Priest, he went on a mission to the Georgia American Colony where his preaching didn't convert too many Native Americans. He later fled back to England to avoid some religious legal troubles.
(see: https://en.wikipedia.org/wiki/John_Wesley and https://en.wikipedia.org/wiki/Methodism)

Later he joined a Bible study group and felt his "heart strangely warmed" by what he was learning there. He soon quit the study group to go preach. His preaching was then very successful for many decades thereafter.

He was a man on fire for God. And people would gather from miles around to see him burn.

In the beginning (1739) Wesley sent lay ministers out to preach and form Methodist Societies in the towns and villages around England. At this point, Wesley was still a Church of England Priest.

The Methodist Society leadership were not ordained ecclesiastical clergy. That didn't happen until some chapel buildings were erected toward 1745. At that time, Wesley officially broke away from the Church of England claiming that the apostolic succession could be transmitted, not only through the bishops, but also through the priests, like himself.

The idea of leading a methodical life of charity toward others was his main mission. But, that was not all.

Look at what John Wesley, founder of the Methodist faith believed happened to the original Church of Jesus Christ and the Apostles' authority?

> (John Wesley in Company With High Churchmen, by H. W. Holden, 1870, pages 57–59)
> "Although he believed in apostolic succession, he also once called the idea of **uninterrupted succession a "fable".**"

It appears John Wesley knew that the uninterrupted apostolic succession of priesthood authority had some missing links in the chain. I assume he learned this about the Church of England's breakaway under King Henry VIII; as John Wesley was an Anglican Church of England Priest.

> (John Wesley - https://gracequotes.org/author-quote/john-wesley/)
> "I learned more about Christianity from my mother **than from all the theologians in England.**"

The theologians at the time were teachers in the main **State Church** of the day in England.

> (Wesley, Sermon 134 , on the importance of doctrine)
> "But how few are these in comparison of **those who adulterate the word of God!** How little wholesome food have we for our souls, and **what abundance of <u>poison</u>**! How few are there that, either in writing or preaching, declare the genuine gospel of Christ, in the simplicity and purity wherewith it is set forth in the venerable records of our own Church! And how are we enclosed on every side with those who, neither knowing the doctrines of our Church, nor the Scriptures, nor the power of God, have found out to themselves **inventions wherewith they constantly <u>corrupt others</u> also**!"

Learning Points:
   A. Wesley felt that many Priests and teachers of religion around him were **poisoning the people with corrupt doctrines**. This was in the 1740s, **before** the American Revolution.
   B. There is the word "corrupt" again. As in corruption of the fruit of the vineyard.

And there is more...Wesley is going to speak directly of the Church of Jesus Christ in ancient times. It isn't pleasant.

> (Wesley, Sermon 134 , on the importance of doctrine)

"How faithful **she** was once to her Lord, to whom she had been betrothed **as a chaste virgin**, let not only **the writings of her sons**, which shall be **had in honour throughout all generations**, but also the **blood of her martyrs**, speak;—a stronger testimony of **her faithfulness** than could be given by words, even

By all the speeches of the babbling earth.

But how is **she now become an harlot**! How hath **she departed from her Lord**! How hath **she denied him**, and listened to the voice of strangers! both,

1. In respect of doctrine; and,
2. Of practice."

Learning Points:
A. John Wesley knew of The Great Apostasy.
B. The **once clean virgin bride** of the church had then **developed into a harlot**. A harlot is another name for a **whore**. John the Revelator and Nephi both wrote about a Whore named: Babylon The Great. (See their writings for information)
C. The writings of the chaste virgin church's sons would be The original 12 Apostles of The Lamb
D. The martyrs of Christianity are from the oppression of Rome under a state religion of idolatry.
E. The 2 problem points that John Wesley illuminates are: 1. doctrine and 2. practice (or ordinances).

John Wesley was onto the mystery. He used his talent for being set on fire in his preaching to alert many people to a need to repent and come unto Christ. And in his day of the 1740s, that was all that could be done.

Thomas Jefferson

My favorite U.S. President is Thomas Jefferson (1743-1826).

As you know from *The "Last Days" Timeline – Volume 1*, I have studied much surrounding the Presidents. The answers to many of our future **3 Eagle Head problems** are found within the writings of Thomas Jefferson. He has foreseen the political problems we would face, and he wrote about **the political solutions**.

(public domain image)

Even Jefferson's nickname by people that knew him closely was "**Old Eagle**."

But politics was not all Jefferson wrote about.

Many say Jefferson was a "Deist"; or someone that believes in a distant God, that set up the Universe but then doesn't interact. (See: https://en.wikipedia.org/wiki/Deism)

There are many sources to prove that idea false:
1. Jefferson loved the words of Jesus Christ. He felt that they were the most sublime words uttered to man. In fact, many modern scholars think he formed "his own Bible." Not true again. I have seen copies of the little book that Thomas

Jefferson made with Christ's words. That is all it is. Just the words of Jesus Christ taken out of the New Testament and condensed so he could read them over and over in several different languages. It was a study technique. The direct words of his Savior.

2. Jefferson toward the end of his life, helped finance and build a Presbyterian Church and a few others. Plus he attended church weekly.

Did Thomas Jefferson Believe in Jesus Christ?

Even in Thomas Jefferson's day, people called him an atheist. Let's have Jefferson speak for himself…concerning his *wee book* of Jesus' teachings.

> (*The Real Thomas Jefferson* by Allison, Maxfield, Cook, and Skousen, page 299 accents added)
> "A more beautiful or **precious morsel of ethics** I have never seen. It is a document **in proof** that **I am a *real Christian***, that is to say, a **disciple of the doctrines of Jesus** – very different from the Platonists, who call *me* infidel and *themselves* Christians and preachers of the gospel, while they draw all their characteristic **dogmas** from what its Author (Jesus) **never said nor saw.**"

And this…

> (*The Real Thomas Jefferson* by Allison, Maxfield, Cook, and Skousen, page 300 accents added)
> "My views of [the Christian religion] are **the result of a life of inquiry** and reflection, and very different from that anti-Christian system **imputed to me** by those who know nothing of my opinions. To the **corruptions of Christianity** I am indeed opposed; but **not** to the **genuine precepts of Jesus himself.** **I am a Christian**, in the only sense in which he wished anyone to be – **sincerely attached** to his doctrines in preference to all others."

What Did Thomas Jefferson Say About *What Happened* to The Original Church of Jesus Christ?

Now let's focus our attention on Jefferson's writings about religion. He had much wisdom in this area.

> (*The Real Thomas Jefferson* by Allison, Maxfield, Cook, and Skousen, page 301 accents added)
> "Happy in the prospect of a restoration of primitive Christianity."

I relish this next brilliant quote out of Jefferson's own lips in 1822, the last few years before his death. Just 8 years before the 1830 restoration of The Church of Jesus Christ to the Earth.

> (*The Real Thomas Jefferson* by Allison, Maxfield, Cook, and Skousen, page 301 accents added)
> "I must leave to younger athletes to encounter and **lop off the false branches** which have **been engrafted into it** by the mythologists of **the middle and modern ages**."

Thomas Jefferson in the last years of his life, spoke of the Church of Jesus Christ **as a tree** that had **false branches grafted** onto it.

He expects one day to have men younger than himself lop the false branches off. And he expected the future people of America to do it. It didn't take long to realize that admonition.

> (Thomas Jefferson November 4, 1820)
> "If **the freedom of religion, guaranteed to us by law** in theory, can ever rise in practice under the overbearing inquisition of public opinion, truth will prevail over fanaticism, and **the genuine doctrines of Jesus, so long perverted by His pseudo-priests, will again be restored to their original purity**. This reformation will advance with the other improvements of the human mind, but **too late for me to witness it**."

Thomas Jefferson knew of The Great Apostasy. He was waiting for Jesus' true religion to be re-established in America, because of the law of the U.S. Constitution.

Jefferson died on the 4th of July 1826. (Just a few hours before John Adams had passed through the veil **on the same day**.) This day being the **exact date of the 50th anniversary of the July 4th 1776, Declaration of Independence** which Jefferson authored.

I see the hand of God in Thomas Jefferson's life. Even the shepherding hand of Jesus was present through Jefferson's life and death. Thomas Jefferson was an important vessel to God in this time of early America.

Jefferson died just four short years before the Church was restored by Joseph Smith Jr. in 1830 **as a young man**. Joseph's foundational preparation work to receive the Book of Mormon plates had already begun in upstate New York in 1820.

Jefferson almost lived to see the restoration of the true church upon the earth. He was very close…and **he knew it.**

In fact, Thomas Jefferson was one of the primary men requesting baptism in the St. George Temple by Wilford Woodruff. (See: *The Other Eminent Men of Wilford Woodruff* by Anderson)

Dr. William Smith

In 1863, one of the first Bible Dictionaries was published to the world by Dr. William Smith.

The original 1863 edition was a full 3 volume set. Printed in London for the old world and in Boston Massachusetts for the new world.

(public domain image)

It was a work of 73 of the most brilliant biblical minds of the times. This bible dictionary greatly helped the advancement of Greek and Latin in religious schools in America and in Europe.
(see: https://en.wikipedia.org/wiki/Smith%27s_Bible_Dictionary and https://en.wikipedia.org/wiki/William_Smith_(lexicographer))

Smith's work toward biblical understanding was paramount in England and earned him knighthood in 1892.

What did Sir William Smith have to say about the original Church of Jesus Christ:

> (Smith's Dictionary of the Bible by William Smith 1896)
> "...we must **not expect** to see the Church of Holy Scripture actually existing in its perfection on the earth. **It is not to be**

found, thus perfect, either in the collected fragments of Christendom, or still less in any one of these fragments…"

The Great Apostasy was real to Sir William Smith. This statement came from a man that spent decades of his life studying the scriptures and making high-quality dictionary books about them; the best of the 1800s.

Dr. Harry Emerson Fosdick

I am no fan of Harry Emerson Fosdick (1878-1969)

The more I read about him, the more I didn't like. A brief synopsis of his preaching and associations:
1. He was born in upstate New York in 1878. Just 45 years after the Prophet Joseph Smith Jr. left there.
2. He became a New York City preacher. Eventually to become one of the largest big city preachers in the nation. **In 1922-1930s he had a nationwide religious radio show**. The same time as when Ezra's Eagle was rising.
3. He would take preaching jobs offered by **different religions** than what he believed.
4. He was funded by **John D. Rockefeller Jr**. who sat in the Park Avenue Baptist Church in New York City.
5. Rockefeller put him on the cover of **Time Magazine**.
6. **Rockefeller heavily pushed** Fosdick's most famous sermon into the public view across the United States. "Shall The Fundamentalists Win?" And they did it under a new less-

(public domain image)

aggressive name "The New Knowledge and the Christian Faith."

(see: http://baptiststudiesonline.com/wp-content/uploads/2007/01/shall-the-fundamentalists-win.pdf and https://en.wikipedia.org/wiki/Harry_Emerson_Fosdick)

    a. In this sermon, **all major parts** of the Gospel of Jesus Christ are harangued and made to look "uncivilized." Including: the virgin birth, the modern theory of evolution is upheld as being from God, the Bible is not the Word of God, rejecting creationism, rejecting the 2nd coming of Jesus Christ, and more.

7. Fosdick's brother Raymond Fosdick was in charge of **John D. Rockefeller Jr's, Rockefeller Foundation for 3 decades**. Starting in 1921. This is directly over the time when Ezra's Eagle was starting up in 1929 and **those funds** were used to put the newly developed 3 Eagle Heads in power behind the feathers.

8. Harry Emerson Fosdick looks like **a religious arm** of John D. Rockefeller. One of the Big 3. (See book: *The President Makers* by Don Fotheringham. My review is here: https://www.LastDaysTimeline.com/president-makers)

When all that is said about Harry Emerson Fosdick, I must ask myself, why would I want to quote him.

The reason is simple: Even people I don't agree with have some truth to their message.

This is what Harry Emerson Fosdick had to say about Christ's original church:

> (Liahona: The Elder's Journal, April 20, 1926, page 424)
> "A **religious reformation** is afoot, and at heart it is the endeavor **to recover** for our modern life **the religion of Jesus** as against the **vast, intricate, largely inadequate and often positively false religion about Jesus. Christianity to-day has largely left the religion which he preached**, taught and lived, and **has <u>substituted</u> another kind of religion altogether.**
>
> If Jesus should come back to earth now, hear the mythologies built up around him, see the **creedalism, denominationalism**, sacramentalism, carried on in his name, he would certainly say, "**If this is Christianity, I am not a Christian.**""

Learning Points:
   A. Dr. Fosdick at the late date of 1926 admitted that the schisms in Christianity are not correct.
   B. The religious reformation is nothing more than an attempt to recover Jesus' religion of the New Testament.
   C. 2 of the 3 problems that Dr. Fosdick has noted are **the creeds** and the multiple **various denominations**. Just as Jesus said when visiting the boy Joseph Smith Jr. in the spring of 1820. Well before, this Rockefeller-loving clergyman was born.

I accept truth from all sources. Even sources I do not like.

Appendix 3: Other Vineyards and Tree Principles in the Scriptures

This appendix section is to show where other vineyards and tree stories happen in the scriptures.

- **D&C 101:43** – This is another Vineyard parable. This one is where the Lord gives some commandments to the servants and the servants don't do it right and the enemy wins (for a while). Then the Lord of the vineyard returns and sets things straight.

  This may **not** have specific reference to the normal Jacob 5 Vineyard Allegory. Unless, this is a temporary setback in the whole Vineyard story, for the time in Jacob 5 when many more servants are called to work in the vineyard.

  Also, In D&C 101:21 – Joseph Smith is identified as "The Man Servant" that the Lord of the Vineyard spake about. And in V22, Joseph is to take the strength of the Lord's house to redeem the Vineyard from the enemy. (ie Jackson County in the Zion's Camp march)

- **Matt 20:1** – This Parable of the Laborers in the Vineyard is classic. It's about timing. The last laborers get the same reward as the earlier laborers. And everyone must be content as that is what the Lord gave as the agreement.

- **Luke 20:9** – The Parable of the Wicked Husbandman – This parable is where the chief Husbandmen of the Vineyard actually kill the Master's son. Yep. This is directed at the leaders of Israel in Jerusalem during Jesus' time. Note: all 3 minor Gospels have this same story in it. Not John. Incidentally, it is included in the apocryphal Gospel of Thomas.

Isaiah 5 - Isaiah`s Vineyard

This allegory is one of the best in the scriptures that match the meaning and outcomes of Zenos' Prophecy of The Tame and Wild Olive Trees.

The meanings of the elements are nearly identical. However, not so plentiful, as in Zenos' prophecy.

Isaiah lived in the 740s B.C. in the Jerusalem area in the Kingdom of Judah **before** the Babylonian captivity. This is well **before** Lehi's time of 600 B.C.

What Lineups Exist Between Isaiah's Vineyard Prophecy and Zenos' Vineyard Prophecy?

The first thing to do before looking at Isaiah's Vineyard Prophecy is to set the stage.

Isaiah's Vineyard Prophecy comes **early** in the Book of Isaiah. It is in Chapter 5. This presumably means that Isaiah received this prophecy early in his ministry.

This may mean that the rest of the Isaiah's imagery and symbols around vineyards and plant-growth could be related to this very early vineyard prophecy. Let's see if that makes sense.

> (Isaiah 5:1-3 accents added)
> "**1** Now will I sing to **my wellbeloved** a song of my beloved touching his vineyard. **My wellbeloved** hath **a vineyard** in a **very fruitful hill**:
> **2** And he **fenced it**, and **gathered out the stones** thereof, and **planted it** with the choicest vine, and **built a tower** in the midst of it, and also **made a winepress** therein: and he looked that it should bring forth <u>grapes</u>, and it brought forth <u>**wild grapes**</u>.
> **3** And now, O inhabitants of Jerusalem, and men of Judah, <u>judge</u>, I pray you, betwixt me and my vineyard."

Learning Points:
  A. This appears to be a song or poetry that Isaiah composed about God's vineyard.

B. In this parable song, Isaiah uses **grapes instead of olives**. This section is about grapes, but the exact same principles are taught about the moving of Israel out of its place as Zenos' Prophecy of The Tame and Wild Olive Trees.
   a. **Author's Analysis:** Remember, the timeframe in which Zenos lived was approximately the same as Isaiah. And these 2 scriptural prophets have very **similar prophetic vineyard prophetic parables**. I believe it would be impossible at this date 2019 to prove which prophet came first. But, they are sharing similar messages at a similar time period. Perhaps in the future, we can narrow down which prophet came first.
C. This parable song was directed toward the Jews in Jerusalem. Not Northern Israel.

Now, let's see more about those "wild grapes." What will the Lord do because of them?

(Isaiah 5:4-7 accents added)
"**4 What could have been done more to my vineyard, that I have not done in it?** wherefore, when I looked that it should bring forth **grapes**, brought it forth **wild grapes**?
5 And now go to; I will tell you what I will do to my vineyard: I will **take away the hedge** thereof, and it shall be **eaten up**; and **break down the wall** thereof, and it shall be **trodden down**:

6 And **I will lay it waste**: it shall **not be pruned**, **nor digged**; but there **shall come up briers and thorns**: I will also command the clouds that they rain <u>no rain</u> upon it.

7 For the **vineyard of the Lord of hosts** <u>is the house of Israel</u>, and the **men of Judah** his pleasant plant: and he looked for judgment, but behold oppression; for righteousness, but behold a cry."

Learning Points:

A. The same cry of "what could I have done more" is the same in both prophecies Isaiah and Zenos.

B. Grapes and Wild Grapes – This time, there was no transplanting of branches that yielded the wild grapes. The **wild grapes of apostasy** came up on their own accord from the natural branches.

C. **Destruction of the vineyard** – It appears because the bad wild grapes came on their own accord, there was no attempt to save the vineyard. It was intentionally destroyed by the master.

D. Pruning and digging – this element is in both prophecies.

E. **Intentional destruction and no rain** – This implies that the master of this vineyard has super natural powers of stopping the clouds from raining. There were no super natural powers attributed to the Master of the Vineyard in Jacob 5.

F. The Vineyard = The whole House of Israel including the Northern Tribes of Israel that became the Lost 10 Tribes. But, yet Judah is defined as the grape vines themselves. NOT the whole of Israel.

Where Does This Prophecy Fit?

The similarities between the writers Isaiah and Zenos are very hard to ignore. It appears that Isaiah had read Zenos' work. **Which would make Zenos' timeframe pre-Isaiah.** At least it seems that way. It is hard to know for sure.

Zenos' prophecy is **very long**. Isaiah's is a **short** 7 verses.

If one were to ask where does this Isaiah vineyard prophecy fit in The "Last Days" Timeline? It would appear to specifically be talking about **Judah's future captivity into Babylon.**

Thus, Isaiah's vineyard prophecy is **limited in scope**. It is not as grand in scope as Zenos' Prophecy of The Tame and Wild Olive Trees recorded in Jacob 5 in the Book of Mormon.

Isaiah's vineyard prophecy **would fit directly at the beginning** of Zenos' olive tree prophecy when the young branches were being moved and the original branches were being burned.

Nephi Included Isaiah 5 as Well…Looking to the Last Days

2 Nephi 15 – Nephi inserted this section of Isaiah 5 in the Book of Mormon small plates. He had a reason to show the timeline of his people and the land of America. Now you know the spot on the timeline that Nephi was quoting. It was all future to him.

The rest of Isaiah 5 that Nephi included was speaking of the destructions Babylon would bring upon Jerusalem and how bad it would get.

Yet, remember the Lord said **Isaiah will be repeated again (see 3 Nephi 1-3)**. So, these things we read about in Isaiah have been fulfilled once. They will be **fulfilled again** in the "last days."

- Isaiah's **Branch, Stem, Root, Rod** etc... these are vineyard symbols. And these are the scriptural names of 4 special last days leaders. The Stem being Jesus Christ himself. (For further research see Appendix of The "Last Days" Timeline – Volume 1: The Branch, Stem, Root, Rod All of Jessie)

- There are Hymns around the "vineyard" topic

- Noah's olive branch to see if it was safe to exit the ark – see also Josephus speaking of the olive branch.

- The Great Seal of The United States of America shows an olive branch in the USA eagle's foot.

Appendix 4: Times of the Gentiles

This section is to show when the Times of The Gentiles **started** and **ends**.

This way, you will know what situations to look toward in the future.

The Beginning of the Times of The Gentiles

In Jesus' day of 33 A.D., the time of the Natural Branches of Israel was coming to a close. The Lost 10 Tribes had already been hidden. The Jewish Natural Branch was in decline and would soon be wiped out in 70 A.D. by the Roman legions attack on Jerusalem and the Temple.

However, Jesus the Messiah had just appeared to the Jews and they rejected him. Not only that, but they have rejected the testimony of their own Jewish born people, the Apostles of the Lamb of God.

So, if the Jews rejected Jesus Christ's true church, then it would be offered to the Gentiles. And the grafting of the wild branches would commence.

Here is the sequence of events:

1. (Acts 4-5) Peter and John were arrested twice. And then they were "let go" and told them not to preach about Jesus.

2. (Acts 6-7) A little later, Stephen had been picked up by the religious police of Judaism. He was brought before the council. Stephen gave a magnificent testimony. However that testimony was a little too heated toward the Jews. And they stoned Stephen to death for that testimony. And Saul/Paul stood by and held the coats so the stoners could do their awful deed.

3. (Acts 9) Saul/Paul is called by Jesus Christ directly to become an Apostle to the Gentiles. But, at this moment, the preaching hasn't opened up yet to the Gentiles. But soon enough.

4. (Acts 10) The **very next chapter**…Cornelius a Roman Centurion that was a devout religious man, received an angel of God. The angel said to seek out the President of the Church Peter in the nearby city of Joppa.

5. (Acts 10) The next day, Peter receives a vision from God of "unclean" animals being let down from heaven. The commandment came to Peter to rise and eat. According to the Law of Moses, these unclean animals were not to be eaten. And Peter knew it. However, the vision was shown 3 times to Peter. Peter knows that anything shown 3 times is

important and he must do. (Peter denied Jesus thrice. Jesus asked Peter to feed His Sheep thrice.)

    a. And immediately, when the vision was over, **a Gentile** man was waiting at the gate of the house in Joppa to escort Peter to Cornelius the Gentile. And Peter baptized the whole house of Cornelius. **The first Gentile to join the Church of Jesus Christ.**

This vision opened The Times of the Gentiles. It was the beginning.

The Times of The Gentiles Starts to Bear Fruit

In Acts chapter 13, Paul is called on his first mission to the Gentiles. And it was successful.

Paul spends the next several decades of his life preaching **first** to the Jews in the synagogues in Asia Minor…**then** when they reject him, he preaches to the Gentiles in those same cities.

And he has much more success among the Gentiles. For whole congregations are established all over Asia Minor…filled with Gentile converts.

The majority of the New Testament is the writings of Paul to those churches that were set up among the Gentiles.

The Fullness of The Gentiles

This phrase is different.

It tells of a time when the Gentiles have expanded the Gospel of Jesus Christ to its maximum size.

The fullness of the Gentiles is when the Gentiles have established much Bad Fruit on the Mother Tree…

…AND when the first few graftings have happened to establish the Church of Jesus Christ among the Believing Gentiles.

This is our time of 2019, in which we live today.

The End of the Times of The Gentiles OR The Times of the Gentiles Have Fully Come In

This is yet future to 2019. This process is described in *The Last Days Timeline – Volume 1*.

Briefly – When the 4th Beast Kingdom is set up by the 3 Awakened Eagle Heads of Ezra's Eagle and that kingdom eventually gets mounted by The Whore Church Babylon The Great as a pseudo-state religion, that is your signal to prepare for what happens next.

The Great Persecution Period comes at this time. At that point, the Times of The Gentiles **is at an end**.

The Unbelieving Gentiles will have officially attacked Jesus Christ's true church that was held out **to them** all the day long through missionary work.

That is the moment when you shall see the Hand of God move greatly **in the believing Gentile's favor** in the Vineyard. For the time has arrived for Israel to obtain its Promised Lands. The **first** Wild Gentile Branch will be removed…to make room for the first Tribe of Israel to be re-grafted in the stead thereof.

Slowly and surely, the rest will follow.

Alphabetized Index

1

144,000, 152, 160, 161, <u>162</u>, <u>163</u>, <u>164</u>, <u>167</u>, <u>168</u>
1820, 89, 90, 91, 93, 97, <u>114</u>, <u>115</u>, <u>116</u>, <u>118</u>, <u>119</u>, 121, 122, 123, 125, <u>134</u>, 141, 142, 219, 220, 225
1830, 44, 138, 141, 142, <u>161</u>, <u>162</u>, 207, 208, 218, 220

4

4th Beast Kingdom of the Gentiles, 84, <u>137</u>, 145

5

5th Seal, 67, 68

6

6th Seal, 68

A

Abraham, 37, 55, 84, 180
<u>accountability</u>, <u>157</u>
Allegory, 16, 19, 20, 25, 227
animal sacrifice, 58
apostle of the Gentiles, 57, 58
Assyria, 24, 28, 29, 41, 48, 75, 181

B

Baal, 22, 24, 55, 56
Babylon, 24, 28, 56, 101, 145, 214, 237
<u>Bad Fruit</u>, <u>77</u>, 83, 90, 92, 93, <u>115</u>, <u>116</u>, 158, <u>171</u>, 172, 237
baptism, 44, 84, 101, 206, 209, 220
Battle of Armageddon, 55, 174
Battle of Gog and Magog, 171, 174
Battle of The Great God, 174
belief systems, 90, 91, 93, 101, <u>106</u>
<u>believing Gentile</u>, <u>104</u>
Benjamin, 42, 55, 56, 73, 74, 103, 143
Bible, 92, 93, 96, 97, 98, 101, 102, 103, 123, 128, 141, 183, 198, 200, 204, 211, 216, 221, 224
Book of Mormon, 119

branches, 23, <u>25</u>, 26, 27, 28, 32, 33, 34, 35, 41, <u>42</u>, 45, 47, 49, 59, 60, <u>61</u>, 69, 71, 73, 76, <u>77</u>, 78, 79, 88, 90, 91, 92, 93, <u>107</u>, <u>115</u>, <u>117</u>, 125, 133, 134, <u>135</u>, <u>136</u>, <u>137</u>, 142, 144, 145, 150, 151, 152, 153, 154, 155, 156, 157, 158, 159, <u>164</u>, <u>165</u>, <u>166</u>, <u>168</u>, 177, 219, 234
Brother of Jared, 156
burned, 26, 27, 28, 35, 41, 42, 93, 121, 133, <u>137</u>, 150, 156, 160, <u>161</u>, <u>165</u>, <u>166</u>, <u>169</u>, 171

C

children of Lehi, 40, 41, 42, 73, 74, 77, <u>108</u>, <u>115</u>, <u>116</u>, 119, <u>137</u>
Christianity, 42, 65, 99, 103, 204, 212, 214, 218, 225
Church of Jesus Christ., 51, 125
<u>corrupt</u>, <u>109</u>, <u>115</u>, <u>116</u>, 120, 123, 125, 127, 128, <u>167</u>, 198, 199, 213
<u>covenant promise</u>, <u>61</u>, *63*

D

Dan, 74, 75, 76
decay, 22, 23, 26, 36, <u>168</u>
decaying, 23
Deliverer, 61, <u>62</u>, *63*
Deliverer of Israel, 62
<u>digging</u>, <u>25</u>, <u>162</u>
Donald Trump, 143

E

Enoch, 158, <u>168</u>
Ephraim, 29, 73, 74, 77, 155, <u>165</u>
Europe, 29, 59, 91, <u>106</u>, <u>115</u>, 122, 153, 155, 158, 197, 221
European, 29, 45, 49, 60, 103

F

<u>Father</u>, <u>7</u>, 14, 31, 33, 34, 36, 37, 38, 39, 40, 41, 43, 44, 49, 79, 80, 81, 82, 83, 89, 90, 91, <u>108</u>, <u>112</u>, <u>116</u>, <u>119</u>, 120, 121, 122, 131, <u>134</u>, <u>138</u>, 139, 142, 143, 144, 145, 149, 150, 151, 153, 157, 158, 161, <u>166</u>, <u>168</u>, <u>169</u>, 172
fertilizer, 25

G

galaxy, 26
Gentile, 29, 35, 45, 46, 49, 53, 54, 55, 58, 60, 65, 81, 84, 86, 87, 90, 92, 93, 94, 102, 104, 108, 121, 125, 131, 133, 134, 137, 138, 142, 144, 145, 150, 152, 153, 155, 156, 157, 159, 160, 161, 162, 164, 165, 166, 169, 176, 236, 238
Gentiles, 17, 19, 20, 28, 29, 35, 37, 42, 43, 44, 45, 47, 49, 50, 51, 52, 54, 57, 58, 59, 60, 61, 62, 63, 65, 68, 80, 81, 82, 83, 84, 87, 90, 91, 92, 93, 94, 95, 96, 97, 98, 99, 101, 102, 103, 104, 105, 106, 113, 115, 119, 122, 128, 133, 135, 137, 138, 145, 150, 152, 153, 155, 156, 158, 161, 162, 164, 165, 204, 234, 235, 236, 237, 238
god of prosperity, 24
god of war, 24, 56
Good Fruit, 35, 37, 39, 47, 77, 86, 119, 138, 170, 171
Government, 24
grafted into Israel, 28, 58, 81
Great Apostasy, 35, 67, 86, 87, 90, 93, 99, 108, 112, 115, 128, 134, 135, 182, 201, 205, 206, 214, 219, 222
Great Awakening, 98, 122
Great Persecution Period, 68, 83, 101, 106, 133, 237

H

harlots, 133
hiding, 41
homosexuality, 24
House of Israel, 23, 84, 105

J

Jackson County, 152, 155, 160, 165, 228
Jacob, 2, 16, 19, 20, 21, 22, 25, 27, 31, 36, 40, 42, 47, 61, 69, 73, 74, 75, 76, 77, 87, 91, 115, 116, 121, 129, 133, 136, 141, 143, 144, 150, 154, 159, 160, 164, 167, 169, 171, 180, 227
Jacob chapter 5, 16, 19
Jerusalem, 42, 43, 51, 59, 79, 80, 143, 152, 165, 228, 234
Jesus, 2, 12, 21, 29, 33, 34, 36, 37, 38, 40, 42, 43, 44, 45, 46, 47, 49, 50, 51, 52, 54, 68, 73, 75, 79, 80, 81, 83, 84, 89, 91, 92, 101, 103, 106, 108, 109, 111, 112, 113, 121, 122, 123, 125, 126, 127, 128, 133, 134, 135, 136, 138, 139, 141, 142, 143, 145, 150, 151, 152, 153, 155, 160, 161, 162, 164, 165, 166, 170, 177, 179, 180, 183, 204, 206, 207, 208, 209, 210, 212, 213, 216, 217, 218, 219, 221, 224, 225, 228, 234, 235, 236, 237, 238
Jewish, 29, 42, 53, 54, 55, 56, 57, 58, 60, 62, 103, 106, 143, 234
Jews, 20, 21, 24, 25, 42, 44, 52, 56, 59, 63, 95, 96, 102, 103, 104, 122, 131, 137, 234, 235, 236
John the Beloved Revelator, 62
John the Revelator, 67, 156, 162, 214
Joseph Smith, 64, 89, 111, 122, 123, 126, 127, 138, 142, 176, 207, 220, 223, 225, 227
Judah, 24, 73, 74, 75, 77, 103, 143, 168

K

Kingdom of Israel, 24, 27, 42, 56, 103, 181
Kingdom of Judah, 24, 28, 42, 103

L

landmasses, 25, 26, 34, 35, 47, 49, 69, 164
latter day, 82
Levi, 42, 74, 75, 76
Lion Kingdom, 62, 162
living prophets, 60
long time passed away, 47, 48, 89
Lost 10 Tribes, 29, 33, 34, 41, 42, 44, 62, 69, 72, 73, 74, 75, 77, 79, 80, 84, 103, 114, 115, 135, 137, 162, 164, 234

M

Manasseh, 73, 74, 77, 138
martyred, 67
Martyrs, 67
Master of the Vineyard, 24, 56, 154
Master/Lord of the Vineyard, 33, 41, 44
Messiah, 20, 21, 25, 54, 58, 79, 234
Millennium, 90, 152, 155, 164, 169, 170, 171, 172, 173, 174, 176
Missionaries, 162, 177
Mormon, 16, 20, 44, 64, 83, 91, 99, 101, 102, 104, 105, 108, 119, 129, 138, 156, 176, 177, 179, 220, 232
Mother Tree, 138, 142, 152, 155, 156, 237

N

natural fruit, 47, 65, 150, 151, 154, 159, 164, 165, 166, 167, 168, 169
Nephi, 19, 20, 33, 40, 43, 77, 79, 81, 92, 94, 95, 96, 97, 99, 100, 101, 102, 104, 105, 108, 110, 129, 134, 179, 180, 214, 229, 230, 232
Nephites, 19, 20, 21, 40, 77, 79, 80, 81, 85, 108, 110, 111, 116, 118, 119
nethermost parts, 33, 34, 35, 41, 115, 136, 137
nourishing, 25, 145, 153

O

Old Testament, 18, 19, 20, 24, 52, 60, 91, 103, 128, 141, 180
ordinances, 44, 96, 97, 98, 121, 134, 210, 214
other sheep, 43, 44, 79

P

Paul, 29, 35, 49, 51, 52, 53, 56, 58, 59, 60, 62, 63, 65, 103, 126, 198, 235, 236
People of Zarahemla, 77
persecution, 65, 66, 67, 103, 106, 110, 124, 125
Plates of Brass, 19
priestcrafts, 82, 83
promised land, 94, 95, 105
Promised Land, 20, 42, 83, 106, 204
Prophecy, 1, 7, 8, 13, 16, 20, 21, 22, 40, 53, 59, 60, 83, 114, 131, 168, 175, 176, 179, 180, 181, 230
prophet, 7, 18, 19, 22, 23, 34, 60, 63, 64, 84, 94, 126, 176, 179, 180
Prophet, 18, 52, 126, 207, 223
Prophets, 161, 206, 209
pruning, 25, 162

R

Reformation, 98
Reign of the Judges, 26
Remnant, 42, 55
resurrection, 58, 112, 113
Roman Empire, 29, 42, 65, 103, 182
Rome, 14, 49, 53, 59, 60, 63, 65, 66, 182, 214
root, 25, 32, 47, 59, 60, 79, 92, 145, 154, 157, 164, 166, 233
roots, 25, 32, 35, 49, 60, 77, 78, 79, 90, 91, 92, 93, 105, 133, 134, 136, 137, 138, 144, 152, 154, 155, 156, 157, 158, 159, 177
Rueben, 72, 73

S

sacrifice of children, 24
scripture roots, 134, 138
scriptures, 2, 8, 10, 11, 13, 16, 20, 34, 35, 40, 44, 49, 52, 53, 60, 92, 93, 96, 100, 103, 138, 145, 156, 157, 166, 222, 227
secret combinations, 83, 156, 197
Servant, 27, 28, 31, 33, 34, 35, 49, 69, 71, 73, 75, 77, 80, 87, 89, 114, 119, 122, 133, 134, 135, 139, 143, 145, 151, 160, 161, 162, 170, 227
spirit children, 26
state religion, 35, 42, 66, 214, 237
stumble, 21, 97, 106
stumbled, 57, 93, 98, 106
Stumbling Block, 94, 95, 96, 97, 104
Stumblingblock, 57

T

taking strength unto themselves, 133, 134
Tame and Wild Olive Trees, 1, 2, 7, 8, 16, 19, 20, 21, 25, 36, 40, 59, 60, 83, 114, 141, 176, 179, 180, 181, 230
tame fruit, 47, 76
The Father, 33, 37, 38, 39, 41, 43, 44, 73, 74, 75, 80, 81, 89, 91, 93, 99, 118, 119, 122, 123, 125, 136, 144, 145, 151, 152, 153, 160, 162, 163, 168, 169, 170, 175
The Root, The Stem, The Branch, and The Rod, All of Jessie, 63
Times of the Gentiles, 29, 44, 45, 54, 58, 60, 62, 137, 138, 145, 152, 237
Timothy, 126, 127, 128
Titus, 42
Top Died, 27
Tribes of Israel, 19, 34, 37, 44, 48, 62, 72, 73, 74, 81, 83, 87, 114, 115, 116, 122, 135, 137, 145, 146, 156, 160, 162, 165, 166, 169
true church, 58, 106, 107, 177, 220, 234, 238

U

unbelieving Gentiles, 84, 99, 101, 155
universe, 26

V

Vineyard Check, 77

W

white robes, 67, 68
Whore Church, 101, 128, 130, 131, 133, 134, 145, 237
wild branches, 47, 88, 92, 164
wild tree, 47
Word of God, 13, 34, 60, 102, 157, 224

Z

Zenos, 2, 7, 16, 18, 19, 20, 22, 23, 36, 52, 53, 60, *63*, *64*, 76, 91, 114, 116, 131, 141, 142, 176, 179, 180, 181, 230
Zion, 62, 84, 143, 152, 153, 155, 156, 158, 159, 160, 162, 164, 166, 167, 168, 169, 176, 177, 207

Study Notes

Study Notes

Study Notes

Study Notes

Study Notes

Study Notes

Study Notes

Study Notes

Study Notes

Study Notes

Study Notes

Discover
The "Last Days" Timeline Series

Go to www.LastDaysTimeline.com

...and more to come.